CRAIGAVON HEAL
Tel: 028 3

GARLAND STUDIES ON

THE ELDERLY IN AMERICA

edited by
STUART BRUCHEY
ALLAN NEVINS PROFESSOR EMERITUS
COLUMBIA UNIVERSITY

A GARLAND SERIES

STRUCTURED REMINISCENCE AND GESTALT LIFE REVIEW

Group Treatment of Older Adults for Late Life Adjustment

STEVEN D. KOFFMAN

GARLAND PUBLISHING, Inc.
A MEMBER OF THE TAYLOR & FRANCIS GROUP
NEW YORK & LONDON / 2000

Published in 2000 by
Garland Publishing Inc.
A Member of the Taylor & Francis Group
19 Union Square West
New York, NY 10003

10   9   8   7   6   5   4   3   2   1

Library of Congress Cataloging-in-Publication Data
Koffman, Steven D., 1948–
       Structured reminiscence and gestalt life review : group treatment of older adults for late life adjustment / Steven D. Koffman.
       p. cm. — (Garland studies on the elderly in America)
       Includes bibliographical references and index.
       ISBN 0-8153-3826-0 (alk. paper)
       1. Group psychotherapy for the aged. 2. Reminiscence in old age—Therapeutic use. 3. Adjustment (Psychology) in old age. 4. Depression in old age. I. Title. II. Series.
       RC451.4.A5 K65 2000
       618.97'689156—dc21   99-055078

Printed on acid-free, 250-year-life paper
Manufactured in the United States of America

Dedication

The idea for this study developed from an unusual interaction I had with my father. When he was in his mid-eighties and Alzheimer's was encroaching upon his mind he ruminated a lot, repeating a few stories from his early years. Like a litany of shame and regret, he often reminisced about having disappointed his own father nearly 80 years earlier. One such day I asked him if he wanted to "play a game" with me. He smiled and said "sure." I asked him to close his eyes and pretend that he could talk to his dad, and that he would be listened to and receive a response. My father broke into great body-racking tears and told his dad how sorry and ashamed he was for losing his new hat when he was a little boy. With my father's eyes still closed, I held him and role played his dad and said, "Son, I see how bad you feel about this. You know, I forgave you all this nearly 80 years ago but it looks like you haven't forgiven yourself." My father said that that was exactly right. I stayed in character and replied, "So, how about letting yourself off the hook? It sure would be a relief to both of us." My father said, "Oh, Okay." He pulled away and smiled. After that, I don't believe that my father remembered that "game" we played at all, his short term memory was, after all, impaired—but for the rest of the day he was less irritable, more active, more sociable, more present with some clarity in the here and now. I wondered to myself if old folks get stuck in their stories because they need somehow to finish with them, find some closure, share them completely with someone else and be validated.

My mother was a story teller, but even moreso, she sang songs and told jokes. She taught me to be unafraid to laugh out loud. She role modeled that it was a good thing to meet new people and hear what they had to say, learn what unique wisdom they might share. She always said, "Don't jump to conclusions about people, you don't know what they might be dealing with—better to find out." Mom encouraged me to find out who I was. She told me that, "You should maybe grow up to be a Ben Casey, a doctor fixing people's brains—and you can start with mine, if you please." She was a brilliant woman, from an earlier era and social strata when women with strong intelligence were discouraged from pursuing any academic or professional path. Both my parents would have loved to be college educated but, as life unfolded for them, they never had the opportunity. I am sure they would have been very proud and pleased to see me graduate with the Ph.D. I say to you mom and dad, this one's for you!!

In loving memory

Jack Koffman   Dorothy Koffman
(1908–1996)   (1911–1996)

How did it get so late so soon?
It's night before it's afternoon.
December is here before it's June.
My goodness how the time has flewn.
How did it get so late so soon?

—Dr. Seuss

Contents

List of Tables

Acknowledgments

How amazing it seems and wonderful it is to have reached this day. I am filled with both a sense of gratitude and of relief. I would like to thank my committee members, Dr. Don Nicholas, Dr. David Dixon, Dr. Sharon Bowman, and Dr. Lambert Deckers for their support and guidance in completing this research. Each has role modeled for me and made unique contributions to my academic, professional, and personal development leading to completion of this dissertation and are very much appreciated. My committee chair, Don Nicholas, has been a patient and steadfastly supportive mentor, encouraging me all along the way.

My thanks go also to Dr. Royda Crose for her commitment of support for my study of older adults. Her advice, feedback, and suggestions on screening protocols, treatment development and methodology have been invaluable. Mark Minear, a longtime friend, also provided an enormously important help to the study providing feedback, guidance, and clarity following the pilot demonstration groups. A special thanks goes to Dr. Jim Jones for his assistance with the statistical analyses and interpretations.

The four persons on my research team, Dr. Alan Burkard, Dr. Michele Juarez-Cullen, Marilyn Michael and Judy Huelette, faithfully attended to the facilitation of the reminiscence groups. They were trustworthy and attentive to details in every manner both foreseeable and unexpected. Judy Huelette was instrumental in many ways, always ready and willing to assist throughout the entire study from its inception to completion. The dependable integrity of these four persons gave me complete confidence that the study's methodology would unfold according to plan.

My friend, Dr. Jay Zimmerman, the Director of Training and my supervisor during predoctoral internship gets a special note of gratitude. His "relentless" support (and great good humor) in the process of completion of the dissertation created the time, space, and impetus for much of the preliminary work on the study. My fellow interns, Margie Nauta and Jenny Spencer were, along with Jay and the rest of the staff at Lucina, a powerful cheering section all throughout that internship year.

To the participants themselves, the retired members of the community, volunteers who maintained faithful commitment to the study, I extend my whole-hearted thanks. I enjoyed our telephone interviews and wish that I could have been personally on hand to hear your stories. Many friends and relatives have been present as a genuine and faithful support system during our Indiana sojourn at Ball State University. You all helped my family keep our perspective during this journey. Thank you.

I have saved the most important acknowledgement for last: my wife, Maureen and children, Orion and BreAnna. For faithfully supporting me through these years of graduate school, for forgiving me times of anxiety and stress, for continuing to count on our love ... I thank you!

For understanding my all-too-often absenteeism as spouse and father, and believing in me through thick and thin, cramped student housing and laundromats, trusting that I would indeed get done with my degree ... I thank you! For your laughter and warmth, frustration and tears, I love and honor you. Now, on with life for us together back in our home in the Pacific Northwest!

Structured Reminiscence and Gestalt Life Review

CHAPTER 1

Introduction

A CONVERSATION

"An *empirical study* of old folks, you say . . . sitting around talking about the good old days? Hmmm, that's nice . . . but what could you possibly learn from that? What's the treatment? What are your dependent variables?"

"I'm looking at the effects of two distinctly different treatments which are applied around the naturally occurring, naturally emerging phenomena in older adults of reminiscence. I'm measuring the impact of the treatments on depression, sense of helplessness, the movement from despair to ego integrity, the congruence of self-concept."

"Hmmm, those are real things to us older folks. Sounds interesting."

WHY LIFE REVIEW?

Counseling Psychologists and other professionals in gerontology often promote and encourage reminiscence because they believe it is, somehow, a "good thing" for old people to tell their stories (Job, 1983; Vickers, 1983). There is something compelling, poignant, and in an ineffable way both important and meaningful about the process. Certain dynamics have been associated with life review: righting of old wrongs, making up with enemies, coming to an acceptance of mortal life, developing a sense of serenity, and feeling pride (DeGenova, 1992). It is appropriate to wonder about potential adaptational significance of the life review on various quantifiable facets of mental health, such as depression (Moody, 1988).

The present analogue study examined the changes in levels of depression and adjustment in late life transitions. The variables of depression, helplessness, despair, and loss of self-concept were measured by pre and post-testing. The independent variables were the three group treatment conditions, a structured reminiscence, a gestalt life review group, and a control group wait list condition.

The participants were older adults, randomly selected and randomly assigned to treatment conditions. The participants were drawn from the pool of retirees, faculty and staff, from Ball State University and additional community residents of the Delaware County community, in and around Muncie, Indiana.

BACKGROUND

Mood disorder (e.g., depression) as a mental health issue continues to be a growing concern, affecting approximately 19% of the U.S. adult population over their lifetime as noted in the National Comorbidity Survey regarding prevalence of DSM diagnoses (Kessler et al., 1994). Within a holistic perspective, mental health is multidimensionally interrelated with cognitive, behavioral, social, affective, and the spiritual components of personality functioning. In a holistic model, therefore, interventions for depression would address all these dimensions (Westgate, 1996).

Seligman (1990) has linked helplessness and hopelessness to the depression of our age. Beck (1967) has noted in depression typical hopeless expressions such as "having nothing to look forward to," "having no goals," "seeing no point in living," and a sense of "futility of life." Carson, Soeken, and Grimm (1988), though not specifically studying depression, found that a sense of life satisfaction and purpose were related to hope (Westgate, 1996).

DEMOGRAPHICS OF THE POPULATION

Historically, people have been described as older adults or senior citizens when they reach retirement age, usually age 65 (Burnside & Schmidt, 1984). Neugarten (1974) posited that, since many people become eligible and choose to retire at ages younger than 65 that age 55 might be a reasonable lower limit. The American Association of Retired Persons (1994) recognizes age 50 as a sufficient determinant for the benefits of membership in their organization. Further determinants of group membership for older adults is the distinction between the cohorts of the young-old (age 55–74), the mid-range old (age 75–84), and the oldest-old (age 85 plus) (Burnside & Schmidt, 1994).

PSYCHOSOCIAL ASPECTS

Older adults in the United States have been living longer and staying healthier (Knight, 1992). Nonetheless, psychosocial aspects of group work with older adults require that group leaders have an awareness of special needs (Toseland, 1995). On the emotional level, preoccupation with death and loss may generate stress related to anxiety and depression. On the physical level, sensory defects and diminished energy of group members may require person specific techniques, continual monitoring, and sensitive response. Group leaders should provide psychological support to increase individual members' confidence and to promote group cohesion. Specific contractual agreements regarding, for example, group attendance and communications may serve to contain older persons' defensiveness and resistance to group process. Clear and consistent communications are crucial in protecting against confusion, hurt feelings, lack of interest or engagement, and generally low self-esteem common in older adults (Burnside & Schmidt, 1994).

In later life, 70% of older adults live with spouses or other relatives. Total isolation is rare. Reciprocal emotional ties suggest a link between social support and longevity. The intact traditional family system confronts and supports major later life adaptational challenges in older members: retirement, widowhood, grandparenthood, illness, adjustment to loss, re-orientation, and reorganization. With or without family support, adults over 65 are the group most susceptible to the distresses of mental illness related to adsjustment issues (Butler & Lewis, 1974).

In the later life cycle stages of "Empty Nest" and "Aging" (Carter & McGoldrick, 1989), there are predictable changes, generational developmental needs, tasks of the family, and clinical issues that may emerge. These are inclusive of maintaining one's own (or spousal) functioning, interests in the face of physiological decline, realignment of marital tasks and roles, issues of aging and death, and the stressful impact of chronic illness upon the family. Dealing with adjustment to retirement, the loss of spouse, siblings, and peers can cause intense stress beyond the scope of habitual coping mechanisms (Walsh in

Carter & McGoldrick, 1989). Depression, despair, helplessness, and loss of self-concept may readily arise as sequela to these losses.

While a multiplicity of approaches exist in addressing these emergent and specific needs of older adults in light of the late life cycle developmental adjustment crises, the focus of this study was on the effects of the life review process (Butler, 1974; Lewis & Butler, 1974). The present study was an empirical investigation of its effects, differentially facilitated in two theoretically different treatment delivery modalities: the structured reminiscence (SRLR) and gestalt life review (GLR) psychotherapy groups.

LOSSES AND ADJUSTMENT

The losses older adults experience may be exacerbated by the suffering due to social isolation and loneliness (Gallagher, Thompson, & Peterson, 1982; Winder, 1978). Maintenance of hope is an important source of support for the individuals. Religious faith and/ or search for meaning often assumes a new and important perspective (Frankl, 1959). Emotional issues of older adults have different meanings than they would otherwise due to the psychosocial stresses surrounding death, loss, and conflicts around mortality issues (Bailey, 1984, Krieger & Bascue, 1975).

Kubler-Ross (1969) identifies five stages of dealing with loss. These are denial, anger and resentment, bargaining to try to postpone the inevitable, depression, and acceptance. The unifying characteristic throughout all five stages is hope, and its maintenance. Various modes of reminiscence, ranging from story telling through art and music therapy, may help facilitate the transition through the stages of acceptance of this loss while engendering hope (Winder, 1978). Life review has, therefore, theoretical as well as practical bases for inclusion in the group treatment of older adults.

In life review, unresolved past issues are identified as well as past developmental failures or successes. Unfinished business may be brought to satisfactory closure, setting the stage for resolution- and renewal of hope, permitting the emergence of new meaning and reinterpretation of one's self-concept. Past and current family relationships play a critical role in the resolution of major psychosocial tasks in later life, such as achievement of ego integrity vs. despair and acceptance of one's own mortality (Erikson, 1963; 1982).

The final developmental life stage/task for older adults is the attainment of ego integrity. This involves finding ways to contribute in a generative sense to a society of which they are still a member. Identity formation is a lifelong process for the individual in relation to society. Past and current familial relationships and one's perceived role in resolving psychosocial tasks of later life all relate to the integrity versus despair issue. These issues pertain to a person's coming-to-grips or acceptance of one's own life (Erikson, 1982).

GROUP PSYCHOTHERAPY

Group psychotherapy is productive in terms of therapeutic outcomes as well as a cost effective form of treatment in addressing the psychosocial needs of older adults (Burnside & Schmidt, 1994; Toseland, 1995). In addressing prevention and maintenance aspects of mental health care in this population, there is a substantial history of research in the efficacy of group psychotherapy as a service delivery model. Much of the research in group life review is qualitative and anecdotal while some provides a more empirical evaluative base (Arean, 1993; Haight, 1992). Evaluating treatments in the spirit of determining the specific range of both predictable benefits and limitations of group work continues to be a legitimate focus of study (Buetler, 1991).

Much of the research on group work with older adults has been conducted by diverse professionals such as geriatric social workers, gerontological nurses, and psychiatrists. Psychologists in gerontology make a unique contribution to the research. The scientific and methodological rigor of researchers in psychology generate an expanded knowledge base which support or disconfirm hypotheses, provide rationales for predicting treatment outcome, and also suggest relevant areas for further study.

TERMS AND DEFINITIONS

Depression. For the purposes of the present study, depression is operationally defined by Yesavage, et al. (1983) as an emotional state characterized by client symptom report of features such as extreme sadness, gloomy ruminations, feelings of worthlessness, loss of hope, helplessness, and apprehension. Depression is, in this study, the construct measured by the Geriatric Depression Scale (Yesavage, et al., 1983).

Congruence. For the purposes of the present study, congruence is operationally defined by Neugarten, Havighurst and Tobin (1961) as a continuum of psychological well being. It describes the extent to which an older adult reports similarity between desired and achieved goals, continuity of positive self-concept, his or her life as meaningful and acceptance of "that which life has been." Congruence is, in this study, the dependent variable measured by the Life Satisfaction Index A (Neugarten, Havighurst & Tobin, 1961).

Ego Integrity. For the purposes of the present study, ego integrity is operationally defined by Boylin, Gordon and Nehrke (1976) as the positive resolution of the final developmental psychosocial life stage task based upon Erikson's (1963) ego integrity concept. Ego integrity, a measure of late life adjustment, suggests older people may achieve a sense of acceptance of their own lives and their mortality- or else they fall into despair. Ego integrity is, in this study, the dependent variable measured by the Ego Integrity Scale (Boylin, Gordon & Nehrke, 1976)

Helplessness. For the purposes of the present study, helplessness is operationally defined by Jones (1977) as a belief schema wherein one's past history is an all important determiner of one's present behavior, and that because something- or someone- once strongly affected a person's life, it should have the same effect indefinitely. It involves denial of responsibility for one's own behavior and is an excuse to avoid adjustment. Helplessness is, in this study, the dependent variable measured by the Irrational Beliefs Test (Jones, 1977).

Life Review. For the purposes of the present study, life review is operationally defined as a naturally occurring, emergent, and universal process in older adults characterized by a progressive return to consciousness of past experiences which is prompted by the realization of approaching dissolution and death and compounded by the inability to maintain the sense of personal invulnerability. Life review functions to keep self-concept competent in dealing with both the environment and personal health concerns while warding off ideas of future deterioration and increased dependence (Lewis & Butler, 1974).

Instrumental activities of daily living (IADLs). For the purposes of the present study, IADL are operationally defined by Mangen and Peterson (1982) as the self-maintenance tasks which a non-disabled person would normally perform for him or herself. They include meal preparation, housecleaning, handling money, shopping, and ability to be mobile in the community (Burnside & Schmidt, 1994). IADL are, in this study, demographic variables measured by the IADL Scale which measures the indicated dimensions of functioning (Mangen & Peterson, 1982).

Developmental tasks. For the purposes of the present study, developmental tasks are operationally defined as responses to normal life stressors that occur throughout life, including the aging process (Burnside & Schmidt, 1994). The conflict that needs to be resolved for maturation, adaptation, and adjustment in older adults is ego integrity vs. despair. Resolution of this developmental crisis will facilitate life satisfaction, acceptance of responsibility for one's life, an intact, congruent personhood, and the growth of wisdom (Erikson, 1963; Green, 1964).

Personhood. For the purposes of the present study, the construct of personhood is defined by Tobin (1991) as those qualities that confer distinct individuality to each person. Personhood may be described as the self that individuals strive to preserve through the losses and adjustments of old age (Tobin, 1991).

Self-concept. For the purposes of the present study, self-concept is operationally defined as how one feels about him or herself and that person's attitudes, values, abilities, and the totality of experience (Burnside & Schmidt, 1994). As a multi-dimensional construct, self-concept manifests in various areas of an older person's functioning both past and current: family, social, relational, career, and physical ability.

Victimization. For the purposes of the present study, victimization is operationally defined by Schwartzburg and Janoff-Bulman (1991) as the "experience of suffering, generally the result of physical and/or psychological loss as a result of ruthless design or incidentally or accidentally, often with feelings of helplessness, powerlessness, and hopelessness." Victims' psychological distress is largely due to the loss of basic assumptions held about themselves and the world (Schwartzburg & Janoff-Bulman, 1991).

Bereavement. For the purposes of the present study, bereavement is operationally defined as the strong emotional reaction that occurs after (or in anticipation of) a loss and entails specific psychological mourning processes of grieving (Conway, 1988). Losses for older adults include, but are not limited to loss of assumptive world, loss of self-concept, and loss related to physical decline and mortality.

RATIONALE

Outcome evidence measuring the effectiveness of the two psychological group interventions, the Structured Reminiscence Life Review (SRLR) and Gestalt Life Review (GLR) and their differential impact on depression and specific late life adjustment issues is essential to determine the actual value of the treatment by these models. In accord with Paul's (1967) often cited schema, the present study is indeed following up on the question of which group treatment will be most effective with this older adult population on specified variables. The results will provide evidence regarding the adequacy of the treatment and suggestions regarding relevance of further study.

PURPOSE OF THE STUDY

The purpose of the present study is, therefore, to evaluate the practical value of the group life review treatments in meeting the stated objectives. The consequences of evaluating the comparative effectiveness of the psychological treatments will result in useful feedback in planning further group psychotherapeutic assessment, intervention, research, and suggested research strategy.

ASSUMPTIONS

1. It is assumed that improvement in the described domains will be a result of their participation in group psychotherapy.
2. The experience of participation in group psychotherapy will effectively provide the participants with positive feedback, reinforcement, encouragement, and social support from the environment and that this will cause improvement in affect, increases in positive self-concept, ego integrity, and belief in competence and self-efficacy.
3. An atmosphere of trust and group cohesion will be facilitated and maintained during the course of the program and this will positively impact the treatment outcomes .

LIFE REVIEW

Butler (1974) has presented life review as an opportunity for comradeship plus the reinforcement of mutual encouragement and social validation. Life review also provides an environment which is supportive of the process of adjustment to changes, significantly decreasing anxiety and somatization symptoms (Butler, 1974). Life review therapy, as a form of the reminiscence process, promotes self-awareness and self-respect even in persons with deteriorated health. Life review is an intense and engrossing activity whose content and process is largely determined by current living conditions.

Life review may serve the purpose of keeping in the foreground the concept of self as competent in dealing with both the environment and personal health concerns while warding off ideas of future deterioration and increased dependence (Molinari & Reichlin, 1985). Other uses of life review include learning about things that people might do differently if they had the chance. This might be useful in psychological interventions which focus on assisting the process of ego integration and the emergence of personal meaning in life (DeGenova, 1992).

Life review techniques can be used with various populations. For community-living and psychologically intact older people, life review can be a valuable adjunct to life planning. For more frail older adult populations, life review can help people come to terms with past activities and relationships in terms of accomplishment and gaining a feeling of having done one's best (Waters, 1990).

Life review potentially has a great benefit to many adults in later life. It extends the process of reminiscence, and facilitates resolution of tasks of acceptance of one's life and death. Conflicts or disappointment in earlier stages which may have resulted in cutoffs or frozen images or expectations can now be considered from a new vantage point at a later life stage or from the point of view of other older adults (Walsh, cited in Carter & McGoldrick, 1989).

DELINEATION OF THE RESEARCH PROBLEMS

Will either of the two theoretically diverse group psychological interventions using the naturally occuring developmental phenomena of reminiscence, differentially facilitated, effectively have an impact on older adults report of depressive symptoms and on specified late life adjustment issues?

Will the post-test means, as reflected by the four dependent variables: 1) depression; 2) congruence of self-concept; 3) belief in helplessness; and 4) ego-integrity be significantly changed by manipulation of the independent variables?

Will the two variations on facilitated life review in the treatment groups as defined by the dependent variables be significantly different from that of the no treatment control group? Will the test results be significantly impacted, differentially, by the main effect of either of the two group treatment models? Do the main effects of treatment of the two experimental groups, differ significantly from each other as a function of treatment modality?

SUMMARY OF HYPOTHESES

The following 16 hypotheses will be examined:

Hypothesis 1a: Structured Reminiscence Life Review (SRLR) group participants in the present study will experience a decrease in depressive symptoms as measured by the Geriatric Depression Scale (GDS).

Hypothesis 1b: Gestalt Life Review (GLR) group participants in the present study will experience a decrease in depressive symptoms as measured by the GDS.

Hypothesis 1c: There will be a statistically significant difference between SRLR and GLR post-test means on depressive symptoms as measured by the GDS.

Hypothesis 1d: The post test means for the treatment groups (SRLR and GLR) will show a statistically significantly greater decrease in depressive symptoms as measured by the GDS than the post-test means of the Wait List Control (WLC) group.

Hypothesis 2a: SRLR group participants in the present study will experience an increase in congruence of self-concept as measured by the Congruence subscale of the Life Satisfaction Index A (LSIA).

Hypothesis 2b: GLR group participants in the present study will experience an increase in congruence of self-concept as measured by Congruence subscale of the LSIA.

Hypothesis 2c: There will be a statistically significant difference between SRLR and GLR post-test means on congruence as measured by the LSIA.

Hypothesis 2d: The post test means for the treatment groups (SRLR and GLR) will show a statistically significantly greater increase in congruence of self-concept as measured by the LSIA than the post-test means of the Wait List Control (WLC) group.

Hypothesis 3a: SRLR group participants in the present study will experience a decrease in belief in helplessness as measured by the Helplessness subscale of the Irrational Beliefs Test (IBT).

Hypothesis 3b: GLR group participants in the present study will experience a decrease in belief in helplessness as measured by the Helplessness subscale of the IBT.

Hypothesis 3c: There will be a statistically significant difference between SRLR and GLR post-test means on helplessness symptoms as measured by the IBT.

Hypothesis 3d: The post test means for the treatment groups (SRLR and GLR) will show a statistically significantly greater decrease in helplessness as measured by the IBT than the post-test means of the Wait List Control (WLC) group.

Hypothesis 4a: SRLR:group participants in the present study will experience an increase in ego integrity as measured by the Ego Integrity Scale (EIS).

Hypothesis 4b: GLR group participants in the present study will experience an increase in ego integrity as measured by the EIS.

Hypothesis 4c: There will be a statistically significant difference between SRLR and GLR post-test means on ego integrity as measured by the EIS.

Hypothesis 4d: The post test means for the treatment groups (SRLR and GLR) will show a statistically significantly greater increase in ego integrity as measured by the EIS than the posttest means of the Wait List Control (WLC).

IMPORTANCE OF THE STUDY

The positive benefits of assessing this program will be to establish a body of empirical outcome evidence. Such evidence, measuring the effectiveness of the group life review interventions in positively impacting the multiple domains of concern in the present study with the older adult population, will be invaluable in determining the actual productivity (or counter-productivity) of the treatment. The results of such a study will provide essential evidence of the adequacy of the two life review group treatment models. The present study is designed and presented in a manner which should readily lend itself to replication with other populations.

LIMITATIONS OF STUDY

Factors of demonstrated import which were excluded from the present study are:

1. Subjects who have been screened out of the life review treatment plan will include those for whom a primary diagnosis indicates major depression, anxiety, or other mood or thought disorders as ascertained by the SCL-90–R (Derogatis, 1994).
2. Institutionalized elderly, those who are unable to perform a minimum of instrumental activities of daily living (Fillenbaum,1988) will be screened from the study.
3. Older adults with severe memory impairment and/or confusion will be screened out as research subjects (Crose, 1996).
4. The degree to which demographic or other variables might predict the criteria of frequency, meaning, or type of reminiscence, are questions which suggest a multiple regression analysis, and will not be included in the present study.
5. Differences between institutionalized (nursing homes, hospitals) and non-institutionalized older adults will not be tested in the present study.
6. Although descriptive demographic data will be collected, differences in age cohort membership, disability, gender, or marital status in life review effects will not be tested in the present study.
7. Limited inclusion of participants who represent diversity populations in the present study suggests that the results would apply only to populations with similar demographic parameters and therefore have limited generalizability.
8. Ethnographic, narrative, interpretive, hermeneutical, and spiritual implications of reminiscence and the life review, suggestive of idiographic qualitative variables, are beyond the scope of the present study.
9. Personal religious expression and validation of faith, or emergence of meaning in life which may manifest differently when facilitated by the structured reminiscence or the gestalt model are not included in the present study.

CHAPTER 2

Review of Related Literature

INTRODUCTION

The examination of pertinent literature established several discrete areas of theory and research which, together, contribute to a more complete frame of reference for the present study on life review. The following is a listing of these pertinent components. The first area recognizes the demographics of aging populations, inclusive of future trends and prevalence of depression. The next related area of the literature review is inclusive of themes regarding issues related to loss and depression. Diagnostic criteria and prescriptive treatment for depression in older adult population are addressed along with issues of development and psychological adjustment in older adults. Specific issues include anticipatory and actual bereavement, and loss of assumptive worlds and of self-concept. Congruence of self-concept and the relationship of the reminiscence function are discussed.

The next area of the literature review describes life review and reminiscence theory, positive and negative reminiscence, reminiscence and self-concept, life review and ego integrity, and research in the life review as an interventive modality. A summary of the research on life review in individual and group psychotherapy with older adults completes this section.

An examination of theory, process, and dynamics of group psychotherapy itself is the next theme addressed in the review of literature. Further, elements of social support for older adults in groups and consideration of countertransference issues with psychotherapy group facilitators is reviewed. This section closes with a review of research in group therapy as an interventive modality with depressed older adults.

The literature review must next look at the established structured reminiscence life review group model, the supporting roles of art and music in structured reminiscence and the training model of group facilitation. This is followed by a review which establishes the experimental Gestalt life review group model. The theoretical foundations and therapeutic approaches of Gestalt psychotherapy are noted. Creativity as an integral component in Gestalt group psychotherapy process is discussed which provides the basis for inclusion of dreamwork and psychodramatic elements in the model. This section of the literature review concludes with the application of the Gestalt model to life review groups, inclusive of treatment strategies, use of awareness enhancing exercises, and preparation of Gestalt life review group facilitators.

The review of literature for the present study is summarized with a proposed synthesis and testing of a new model, the Gestalt life review group. Its effectiveness will be compared against that of an already existent group model, the structured reminiscence life review group, across a number of variables of interest, in a theoretically derived, replicable study.

DEMOGRAPHICS

Demographics of Aging Populations

The population of older persons in the United States is growing at a more rapid rate than other segments of society (U.S. Bureau of the Census, 1994). This growth is expected to continue into the 21st century. The "graying" of the American population has led to dramatic increase in programs and services for older persons wherein group work is used extensively (Toseland, 1995).

The older American population, consisting of persons aged 65 or older, numbered 33.2 million in 1994, which represented 12.7% of the U.S. population. The number of older Americans increased by 2.1 million, or 7% since 1990, compared to an increase of 4% for the under age 65 population (AARP, 1995). In 1994, the total percentage of older adults (aged 65+) in the minority population of Americans was 14%; 8% African American, 4% Hispanic, 2% Asian or Pacific, less than 1% Native American (AARP, 1995)

According to 1990 information, 1.6 million, or 5% of 65+ population lived in nursing homes. The percentage increased by age: 65 - 74 = 1%; 75 - 84= 6%; and 85+ = 24%. The majority (68%) of older non-institutionalized persons lived in a family setting. More than 10.4 million or 81% of older men and 10.4 million or 58% of older women lived in families. About 13% (5% men, 17% women) were not living with a spouse but with children, siblings, or other relatives. About 30% of non-institutionalized older persons (9.3 million) lived alone, representing 40% of older women and 16% of older men (U.S. Bureau of the Census, 1994; AARP, 1995).

In 1994, there were 735,000 residents of the State of Indiana who were aged 65 and over. This constituted 12.8% of the state's total population and was a 5.8% increase from 1990. In comparing Indiana with total U.S. census data, in 1994 there were 33,158,000 residents of the United States who were aged 65 and over. This constituted 12.7% of the nation's total population and was a 6.7% increase from 1990 (AARP, 1995).

Activities of daily living statistics are noteworthy demographics as well. Based on data from U.S. Department of Health and Human Services, in 1986, about 6.1 million or 23% older people living in the community (non-institutionalized) had health related difficulties with one or more activities of daily living (ADL) (18% men, 26% women). In excess of seven and one-half million persons (28%) had difficulties with one or more instrumental activities of daily living (IADL). Most who had difficulties with IADL (e.g., bathing, dressing, eating, transferring from bed to chair, walking, getting outside, and using toilet) were receiving some personal help. ADL include preparing meals, shopping, managing money, using telephone, and doing housework (AARP, 1995).

Future trends. The older population will continue to grow in the future (U.S. Bureau of the Census, 1994). The most rapid increase is expected between the years 2010 and 2030 when the "baby boom" generation reaches age 65. By 2030, there will be about 70 million older persons, more than double the 1990 figure, and 20% of the American population. Minority populations are projected to represent 25% of the elderly population in 2030, up from 13% in 1990. The white non-Hispanic pop 65+ is projected to increase by 93% compared with 328% for older minority persons, including Hispanics (555%), African Americans (160%), Native Americans (231%) and Asians and Pacific Islanders (693%) (AARP, 1995).

The conclusions of the National Comorbidity Survey (Kessler et al., 1994) suggest that the majority of persons with psychiatric disorders fail to obtain professional treatment. Whether this is due to obstacles in accessing information, obtaining medication or psychotherapeutic treatment, the results certainly support the development of more outreach programming. In the case of older adult populations, where risk factors (such as social isolation, loss, etc.) of affective disorders such as depression are significantly high, program development with group psychotherapy component is legitimately needed.

Prevalence of depression. In terms of epidemiology, approximately 3% of elderly individuals living in the community meet criteria for major depression. Between 10 and 14% have chronic and sustained depressive symptoms. Approximately half of older patients seen for medical care of physical ailments have significant depressive symptoms and 15% meet criteria for severe clinical depression. Depression in late life is not exclusively associated with excessive stress or adverse life events, often presenting in the absence of any clearly identifiable precipitant cause (Ham & Meyers, 1993).

Slater (1995) refers to the psychology of the aging experience and prevalence of depression. Depression with older adults is a common problem but is often either missed or untreated. Often the symptoms are dismissed as crankiness or moods of old age. Symptoms include 'empty' feelings, ongoing sadness and anxiety, fatigue and sleep problems, eating and weight problems, difficulty concentrating, thoughts of death or suicide (National Institute on Aging & National Committee to Preserve Social Security and Medicare, 1994).

Primary depression occurs in people who have generally been well but who show symptoms of depression in response to events beyond their control. Examples of such events are death of a friend, sudden illness, or a chemical imbalance in the brain. Sixty to eighty percent of depressed older adults are treated successfully as outpatients with either individual or group, anti-depressant medication, or some combination (National Institute on Aging & National Committee to Preserve Social Security and Medicare, 1994).

LOSS AND DEPRESSION

Diagnostic Criteria For Depression

The following dimensions of life functioning are included in the DSM-IV as indicators of depression (APA, 1994). They include loss of interest or pleasure in most or all usual activities plus at least four of these symptoms, for at least two weeks duration:

1. changes in appetite or weight, with either appetite loss or bingeing.
2. disturbed sleep, with either insomnia or hypersomnia.
3. motor agitation or retardation.
4. fatigue or loss of energy.
5. feelings of worthlessness, self-reproach, or excessive guilt.
6. pervading hopelessness, suicidal thinking or attempts.
7. confusion, difficulty with thinking or concentrating.

In older adult populations, depression might appear differently. For example, sadness of mood is present but it may be masked by other symptoms. Impairment in cognition may be marked and even dominate. Confusion may therefore present as dementia. Psychosomatic tendencies, such as aches and pains, or ruminative fears about physical well being may predominate (Ham & Meyers, 1993).

Possible distinctions between clients' reports of symptoms of normal grief and clinical depression (Wolfelt, 1988) are also contrasted in table 1.

Prescriptive treatment. Depression, depending upon its clinical presentation of symptoms, may be treated effectively using a variety of approaches. Psychotherapy, individual and/or group, is effective in alleviating depressive signs and disorders with many older adults. Although antidepressant medications alone are effective with many older adults with severe clinical depression, the combination of medication with some form of cognitive psychotherapy is legitimately prescriptive. If an older adult presents with a chronic history of depression, a family history of affective disorder, acute somatic signs, or problematic comorbidity, medical referral is appropriate. In situations with an assessed high risk of suicidality, whether ideation alone, or history of threats, gestures, or attempts, then referral to a psychiatrist is also indicated (Ham & Meyers, 1993). In a meta-analytic review of group psychotherapy interventions with older adult clients

(Gorey & Cryns, 1991), good support for treating depression using life review groups is suggested.

Table 1: Diagnostic Guidelines: Symptoms of Normal Grief vs. Clinical Depression

	Normal Grief		Clinical Depression
1.	Responds to comfort and support.	1.	Does not accept support.
2.	Often openly angry.	2.	Irritable and may complain but does not directly express anger.
3.	Relates depressed feelings to loss experienced.	3.	Does not relate experiences to a particular life event.
4.	Can still experience moments of enjoyment in life.	4.	Exhibits all pervading sense of doom.
5.	Exhibits feelings of sadness and emptiness.	5.	Projects a sense of hopelessness and chronic emptiness.
6.	May have some transient physical complaints.	6.	Has chronic physical complaints.
7.	Expresses guilt over some specific aspect of the loss.	7.	Has generalized feelings of guilt.
8.	Has temporary impact upon self-esteem.	8.	Loss of self-esteem is of greater duration.

Note. Adapted from: A.D. Wolfelt (1988). *Death and Grief: A Guide for Clergy.* Muncie, IN: Accelerated Development, Inc. Publishers.

Developmental and Adjustment Issues of Older Adults

Older adults encounter stressful life events and must address difficult emergent adjustment needs (Gilewski, Kuppinger, & Zarit, 1985). Unexpected situations and life threatening illness intrude into their established lifespace (Goldmeier, 1985). Emergent crises, such as the diagnosis of illness and subsequent loss of health and abilities, have impact in multiple psychosocial dimensions of functioning for older adults (Beaulieu & Karpinski, 1981).

Accustomed working roles and self concept roles are effected by the life changes (Gilewski, Kuppinger, & Zarit, 1985). In a marriage, for example, long standing and seemingly unchangeable power sharing, instrumental, and caretaking roles may be effected by irreversible second order systemic changes which emerge from change and loss (Beckham & Giordano, 1985). Older adults' assumptive worldviews, religious beliefs, feelings of invulnerability, and sense of security and justice are often shaken to their foundations. Loss of control, loss of hope, loss of health, loss of future may all contribute to not only anticipatory grieving (Conway, 1988), but may complicate real bereavement processes with hopelessness and depression (Taylor, Lichtman, & Wood, 1984). A foundation for addressing the concerns of the target population is established by looking at the factors affecting loss of control and assumptive world views.

Damage to self-concept in the present often isolates the older adult from much that may give them strength and peace. In the late life stage that they are part of, the normal developmental task that must be addressed is that which may be resolved in either a sense of ego integrity or despair (Erikson, 1982). The psychological well being of a grounded ego integrity would include an acknowledgment and remembrance of their past life experiences together, including children and family, work and career accomplishments, social concerns, sense of place in the generations that have gone before and caring for those yet to come, and acceptance of their mortality. The loss of physical health with increased dependence on the medical establishment, often contributes to the loss of autonomy, personal meaning, and/or religious faith (McCarthy, 1985).

Combined with potential unwillingness to explore whole life meaning, inclusive of past histories and self-concept, the older adult may be unable to address unresolved life issues, and unfinished business in their own families and the marriage relationship (Lewis & Butler, 1974). These areas, accessible only through memory and reminiscence, if unacknowledged, will often preclude if not completely block, the honest communication necessary in order that the older adult move through this transition towards acceptance (Gilewski, Kuppinger, & Zarit, 1985).

Coleman (1994) examined psychological adjustment in later life and describes how older adults adjust to the awareness of being in the last stage of life and how they cope with change and loss. The relationship between demoralization and depression is explored in the context of the meaning that these states have for the elderly. Erikson's concept of the last stage of development: integrity vs. despair is discussed. This includes an acceptance of one's life and the way that it has been lived.

A major task facing traditional couples occurs upon a husband's retirement. The adjustment issues surround the husband's incorporation inside the home and include change in age-role expectations, quality of spousal interaction, and relationship intimacy. Initial sense of loss, disorientation, and loneliness contribute to increase in death and suicide rates in the first year following retirement. Loss of congruence of past and current self-concept is a central theme (Lewis, 1971).

Erikson's (1969) final developmental life stage/task, the resolution of despair towards ego integrity is noted as the ground wherein reminiscence may emerge for dealing with unfinished business. Resulting from reminiscence, clients may move adaptively towards integration and resolution of their problems (Carlson, 1984).

In summary, old age is a time wherein unique developmental work can be accomplished. The adaptational tasks of the elderly are inclusive of maintaining self-esteem while adjusting to declining physical health, parallel losses in physical and mental capacity, assumptive worlds, self-concept construction and in relationships. Older adults must cope with grief and depression and hopefully feel they have (and are still) contributing to society (McMahan & Rhudick, 1964). Life review therapy is an effective change agent in process toward this work (Carlson, 1984).

Bereavement and anticipation of loss. The process of psychotherapeutic involvement with depressed and grieving older adults covers the range of supportive interventions through crises, and assessment for potential pathological grieving and adjustment problems (Conway, 1988).

Bereavement can be described as the strong emotional reaction that occurs after a loss and entails specific psychological mourning processes. This is in contrast to anticipatory grief which includes losses already experienced along with those which are impending (Worden, 1982). These losses include loss of physical condition, loss of roles in family, work, and social life, and loss of future life "milestones." Most significantly consuming is the grief over the loss of close relationship, which in elderly couples often is inclusive of a lifetime of mutual support and intimacy, shared struggles, and experience (Conway, 1988).

Open communication is another important determinant in adjustment. Open communication allows the experience, expression, and validation of feelings with each other. An environment of this nature is conducive to addressing unfinished business. Older adults may work through old issues and come to some resolution which is preparatory for further acceptance of the life changes that they must inevitably face.

When the members of a marital dyad differ significantly in their rates of anticipatory bereavement, the gap between these two positions may make genuine sharing and acknowledgment of feelings all but impossible (Conway, 1988). An example cited was descriptive of this kind of communications impasse. Conway reported a case where one spouse who was dying of cancer wanted to talk about his wish to end the struggle. The wife, who was fighting with all her energy to save her husband's life, would not tolerate any discussion, or acknowledgment of impending death. In Life Review groups, windows of opportunity are opened for acknowledgment of feelings of depression, loss, and sadness as well as opportunities for dealing with unfinished business or expressing love and validating intimacy in the present (Feil, 1993).

In any individual elderly client, all forms of reminiscence may be intermingled. Storytelling, positive evaluative life review, and defensive (or fabricated) recall may emerge alternately. By encouragement of clarification of extremes (with both positive and negative associated affect) in recalled events, it may be possible to move beyond obsessive ruminations and more alternatives become available. Implications of the importance of reminiscence and mourning on developmental transition are discussed. Mourning of lost sources of validation is viewed as an essential component of counseling. The process of reminiscence should help people find and recognize new sources of validation, available in the present. (Viney, Benjamin, & Preston, 1989).

Loss of assumptive worlds and self-concept. The experience of older adults who are confronted unexpectedly with a variety of losses (e.g., death of a spouse, life threatening or debilitating illness) may find their assumption of the world as a fair place violated. They may see themselves as being victimized, with the security and sanctity of their lifelong values, worldview, and self-concept irreversibly challenged if not changed.

A myriad of events occur around and to older adults that can be experienced as, in some sense, intrinsically unfair, beyond their control or influence. It is not surprising that helplessness and loss of hope would occur as a consequence . These loss-related events precipitate a shattering of assumptions about oneself in the world (Thompson & Janigian, 1988). As these events may undermine worldview, behavioral patterns, and cognitive schema, these negative events tax coping skills, psychological adjustment, and sense of meaning (Taylor, 1983).

A belief in a just world is a belief that good things happen to people who do good things and bad things happen only to people who do bad things. The belief that everyone gets what they deserve eliminates the necessity for concern and worry over the possibility that aversive events may occur at any time by chance. As the severity of the consequences of an experience of perceived victimization increase, so too will the tendency to assign blame. If this were not the case, then people would have to accept the uncomfortable notion that some major catastrophe may befall them by chance (Langer, 1977; Taylor, 1983).

Common emotional reactions to victimizations include helplessness and depression. Being a victim forces people to confront their assumptions and expectations they have held about themselves and about the world. These schema, adhered to and treasured for a lifetime as raison d'être, may be severely challenged and may no longer be viable. Basic assumptions are often shattered by the extremity of experience. Perceptions and worldview are changed by threat, insecurity, danger, and self-questioning.

Older adults have relatively unique conceptual systems, developed over time, which provide them with viable expectations about themselves and their relationship with their environment. The need to seek meaning is a salient reaction to victimization (Janoff-Bulman & Wortman, 1977).

The need for meaning may well represent a powerful human motivation. Finding a purpose in the perception of one's victimization is one way of coping with a world that makes little or no sense (Frankl, 1959). Older adult "victims" may be prone to see themselves as weak, helpless, frightened, needy, and out of control. Such negative self concept images as these are counter to normal self concepts of people as worthy, positive, and decent people.

The experience of victimization leads to a serious questioning of these established self-perceptions. Victims usually experience a profound threat to their sense of personal autonomy. They find themselves as being powerless in the face of forces beyond their control. The coping and adjustment process involves re-establishing a conceptual system that will allow the victim to once again function effectively. This process involves a new coming to terms with a world in which bad things can and in fact do happen. Part of this working through includes establishing a view of the world as not wholly malevolent and threatening.

The decline of physical health, loss of actual physical capabilities and roles, loss of spousal reciprocity, and loss of accustomed manner of intimacy are blows that require integration and resolution if generativity is to continue rather than hopelessness and despair. Significant impacts on relationships are inextricably connected with impact on identity and may either be remediated or lost altogether (Molinari & Reichlin, 1985).

Congruence of self-concept. Life philosophies and religious schema may also influence a person's appraisal of a recalled past or current adjustment issue. People with a philosophy of all things working out for the best will perceive or remember the same situation differently from someone with a differing worldview. Self schemas are also a relevant variable in the appraisal process. Persons with characteristically strong self-efficacy, who see themselves as people who "can handle whatever comes along" will respond differently from people whose self schema might be "I can't handle unexpected crises at all" (Wortman, 1983, p.210).

Older adults with the personality trait of hardiness are able to appraise stressful events, or reminiscence more optimistically than non-hardy people. Hardiness has three distinguishing characteristics which have potential impact on adjustment to victimizing events. The first is the internalized commitment and behavioral tendency to involve oneself, proactively, in whatever comes along. The tendency to believe that one can influence his or her environment or retain control also has a significant effect, that of empowerment. Thirdly, the belief that change rather than stability is normal in life and that changes represent opportunities or even challenges for growth rather than threats to security can effectively prime a person for life's stressful emergencies (Wortman, 1983).

Self-concept, loss, and reminiscence function. Mourning and reminiscence were studied as parallel psychotherapeutic processes for older adults by Viney, Benjamin, and Preston (1989). They begin with the premise that there are many losses which elderly people face: loved spouses, friends, pets, home, abilities, roles, values, health, and strength. Because of these losses, any psychotherapy for this population needs to be aware of mourning and reminiscence as part of the grieving process. Life review is noted as having therapeutic value. When external sources of validation fail (or are not present) clients turn to their own resources or reminiscence for validation (Viney, Benjamin, & Preston, 1989).

LIFE REVIEW

Old age is a period in which unique developmental work can be accomplished. Life review therapy is an effective means of effecting movement in this domain (Butler, 1974; Hargrave & Anderson, 1992; Lewis & Butler, 1974). Research indicates that life review is a personal, self-evaluative form of reminiscence with interpersonal and intrapersonal dimensions. Exhaustive empirical documentation is lacking regarding the efficacy of life review groups. Butler (1974) has defined life review as a naturally occurring and universal process characterized by a progressive return to consciousness of past experiences which is prompted by the realization of approaching dissolution and death, and compounded by the inability to maintain the sense of personal invulnerability. Certain past experiences must be examined and resolved or at the very least acknowledged for old age and death to be met in an adaptive manner (Molinari & Reichlin, 1985).

Life review groups for the elderly provide the opportunity for comradeship plus the reinforcement of mutual encouragement and social validation (Lewis & Butler, 1974). They also provide an environment which is supportive of the process of adjustment to changes, and to significantly decrease anxiety and somatization symptoms. Reminiscence therapy promotes self-awareness and self-respect even in persons with deteriorated health.

Life review is an intense and engrossing activity whose content and process is largely determined by current living conditions. It may serve the purpose of keeping in the foreground the concept of self as competent in dealing with both the environment and personal health concerns while warding off ideas of future deterioration and increased dependence (Molinari & Reichlin, 1985).

A potential effect of positive reminiscence involves the consolidation of self identity in the face of changes that are inherent in the aging process (Butler, 1974; Molinari & Reichlin, 1985). The decline of physical health, loss of actual physical capabilities and roles, and loss of spousal reciprocity and accustomed manner of intimacy are blows that require integration and resolution if generativity is to continue rather than hopelessness and despair. Significant impacts on relationships are inextricably connected with impact on identity and may either be remediated or lost altogether.

Reminiscence may serve a function similar to mourning (Carlson, 1984). It can result in an ability to acknowledge and grieve what has been lost. A continued wish to return to an idealized past prevents one or both spouses from separating their dependence on the way things were in the past. If this can be resolved then it becomes possible to freely enjoy the memories of the past while living as fully in the present, limitations and changes notwithstanding (Berlatsky, 1962). Life review can occur or be initiated at many transitional periods life crisis. It is most common in the elderly in the face of approaching dissolution and death (Molinari & Reichlin, 1985).

The most important distinction made in the theoretical literature is that Life Review is but one distinct form of the broader construct of reminiscence. In contrast to simple storytelling, Life Review is more personal and intense, often including the process of "grappling" with unresolved life issues or unfinished business (Coleman, 1974). Certain past experiences must be examined and resolved, or at the very least acknowledged, for old age and death to be met in an adaptive manner. Conflict is viewed as a necessary component for resolution to occur.

It is noted in one study (Noyes & Kletti in Molinari & Reichlin, 1985) that in persons of all ages, not just with elderly, an encounter with life threatening danger may precipitate life review process. It is suggested by the authors that intense transitional periods or life crises may initiate the life review process. Also suggested are the possibilities that certain sensory stimuli may have an effect on the emergence or facilitation of life review. Some of these dimensions include visual or auditory components. These may have an influence on the vividness and retrieval of memories (Molinari & Reichlin, 1985).

Life Review and Reminiscence Theory

Reminiscing is defined as the act or habit of thinking about or relating past experiences, especially those considered most significant (Wolinsky, 1986). Reminiscence provides a framework for assessing adjustment and resolution of conflicts in terms of specific developmental stages for both individuals and married couples (McMahan & Rhudick, 1964).

Older adults must find ways of coping with grief and depression resulting from personal losses as well as finding ways to contribute in a generative sense to a society of which they are still members . This is in accord with Erikson's position that identity formation is a lifelong process for the individual and couple in relation to society. Butler (Lewis & Butler, 1974) noted that older adults have the need to review their life preparatory to death and that reminiscences serve to provide the material necessary for this review.

Negative and positive reminiscence. Some life reviewers have seemed preoccupied with the need to justify their lives and the reminiscence reflected themes of guilt, unrealized goals, and wished for opportunities to make up for past failures (McMahan & Rhudick, 1964). Other subjects responded to the task very differently and actively. These were individuals who could be described as storytellers who, with evident pleasure, recalled past exploits and experiences in a manner that was both informative, and entertaining. Those who were able to reminisce actively showed no need to glorify the past while diminishing the experience in the present. Older adults' knowledge and memories provide a unique opportunity and the perspective necessary to preserve self-esteem and maintain a way to contribute to present society in a meaningful way.

Reminiscence is an important means of adjustment to late family life cycle crises. This process is positively correlated with successful adaptation to old age through the maintenance of self-esteem and by reaffirming the sense of identity development. Acknowledging and working through personal losses and changes along with contributing positively to society may be of significant value in maintaining freedom from debilitating depression, pathologic mourning, and to personal survival itself (McMahan & Rhudick, 1964).

There are a variety of types of reminiscence, some more conducive to adjustment and adaptation than others. Storytelling serves the functions of enhancing self-esteem and creating a kind of generative oral history (Bumagin & Hirn, 1989). This is an informative and pleasurable kind of recollection. Some reminiscence provides material directly for the life review process (Butler, 1974; Lewis & Butler, 1974). This is more evaluative in nature and often includes genuine self-scrutiny. This is differentiated from defensive reminiscence or that which glorifies the past while depreciating the present. This is a form of negative life review which may also be framed as obsessive reminiscence, often founded in guilt and depression (Molinari & Reichlin, 1985).

In contrast to simple storytelling, life review reminiscence is personal and intense, representing an "active grappling with the past in order to come to terms with it" (Molinari & Reichlin, p. 82). Both intrapersonal conflicts and conflicts between spouses are viewed as natural and appropriate material which arise in the life review process. Life review can be globally defined as that form of reminiscence in which the past is actively evaluated and wherein conflict is an integral component if resolution of unfinished business is to occur (Butler, 1974; Lewis & Butler, 1974).

Reminiscing has adaptational significance for the needs of older adults in maintaining self-esteem in the face of declining physical health and losses in mental capacity. Coping with grief and depression and finding some sense of contributing to society are also tasks of the elderly. McMahon and Rhudick (1964) defined reminiscing as the act of relating personally significant past experiences. The authors suggested that reminiscing has adaptational meaning. The aged person has a need to review his/her life preparatory to death and reminiscence provides the material for this process (McMahan. & Rhudick, 1964).

Storytelling was observed to fall into three general categories. One type of reminiscence compared present life negatively with past memories of experiences. This seemed to maintain a quality of positive self-esteem. Others engaged in reminiscence behaviors which suggested obsessive rumination, regret, or guilt about the past. Others were described by the authors as entertaining and informative storytellers, using stories of the past to evoke pleasure in both memory and present experience. This third group seemed to have no need to devalue the present or overstate the qualities of the past in the process of active reminiscence. Older person's "knowledge of a bygone era" may allow an opportunity for contribution to the quality of present life while preserving self-esteem through active reminiscence (McMahan & Rhudick, 1964).

Reminiscence provides a framework for assessing both adjustment and the resolution of conflicts in terms of the specific developmental stage for older individuals. Elderly persons must find ways of coping with grief and depression resulting from personal losses as well as finding ways to contribute in a generative sense to a society of which they are still members. This is in accord with Erikson's position that identity formation is a lifelong process for the individual in relation to society (McMahan & Rhudick, 1964).

Positive reminiscence may facilitate the consolidation of self identity in face of changes inherent in the aging process. This resolution may result in the ability to acknowledge and grieve what has been lost. Life reviewers engaged in positive reminiscence also enjoy the memories of the past while living as fully in the present, limitations and changes notwithstanding. The older person's knowledge of a bygone era may even provide the ground or opportunity for societal contribution. In summary, positive reminiscence supports quality of present life while preserving self-esteem (Carlson, 1984).

Reminiscence and self-concept. Carlson (1984) noted that elderly people who frequently reminisce show increased consistency between past and present self-concept when stress is a present life factor. The occurrence of retirement and the emergence of life threatening illness in a marriage are two examples of such stressors and self-concept is uniquely vulnerable to change at such a time. A strong interrelationship between frequency of reminiscence, positive affect while reminiscing, and good personal and social adjustment has been noted. In another study depression was linked to infrequent reminiscence (Carlson, 1984).

Unsuccessful life review, characterized by the more obsessive or ruminating variety of reminiscence, is more commonly found in elderly individuals who had been institutionalized, separated from their spouses or families. These institutionalized elderly were seen as lacking the opportunity to resolve the conflicts and old business that normally arise in the course of reminiscence (Lewis & Butler, 1974).

Lewis (1971), in one of the earliest studies of life review, looked at relationships in reminiscing and self-concept in old age. Subjects were 24 Caucasian males from New England. The participants were given two sets of 48 item Q-sorts, one for their present self-concept and one set for their past self-concept. Subjects were seen again two weeks after the Q-sort experience and had their opinions challenged. Those who had exhibited more reminiscence behavior and whose past self-concept was more consistent with present avoided the influence of stress on their self-esteem.

That life review occurs in old age and is motivated by emergent emotional needs had not yet been researched to any extent. Lewis discussed the implications old age had on self-concept. Consistency of self-concept was noted as adaptive and healthy at the same time as discrepancy between one's past and present self-concept is inevitable. Reminiscence is noted as a means to maintain integrity of the self-concept. Lewis noted that threats to self-concept are predictable with the occurrence of the various losses implicit in aging. Some of the losses made explicit were those of significant life supports such as occupational identity, death of irreplaceable loved ones, and decline in physical abilities (Lewis, 1971).

Life review and ego integrity. Taft and Nehrke (1990) examined the relationship between the frequency of reminiscence and ego integrity and found that these two specific variables were not significantly related. However, the use or purpose of life review, regardless of the frequency, is found to be a mediator of ego integrity for elderly clients. The design of this study was the development of a correlational matrix, using a random sample of institutionalized elderly (N=30) composed equally of males and females. (Taft & Nehrke, 1990).

The measures used are of interest. The Reminiscence Questionnaire (Romaniuk & Romaniuk, 1981) is a 13 item scale with three subscales based on a factor analysis. The factors found in reminiscence are teaching/ entertaining, problem solving, and life review. The Ego Integrity Scale (Boylin, Gordon, & Nehrke, 1976) is a 10 item scale based on Erikson's descriptions of the two poles of the last stage of life development: integrity versus despair. The scales described in this study are, perhaps, the most relevant in terms of future research with life review and in terms of scale development research (Taft & Nehrke, 1990).

Research in the Life Review

Molinari and Reichlin (1985) reviewed the then existent literature on research into Life Review. The authors critique theoretical models, research design, and general trends in the research. Life review was seen as having both interpersonal and intrapersonal dimensions. The Life Review varies as a function of institutional or independent living arrangements for the elderly. Empirical research regarding psychotherapeutic outcome for Life Review groups was lacking. Butler's perspective on the issue was reiterated: that Life Review is a naturally occurring mental process of reminiscence which is characterized by return to consciousness of past experience. This process is facilitated by an increased awareness of one's mortality and loss of a sense of personal invulnerability. It is adaptive for these memories to be brought to light, resolved, and integrated (Molinari & Reichlin, 1985).

A study by DeGenova (1992) had as its premise the life review work of Butler and Lewis. Some of the positive outcomes of life review were described as "righting of old wrongs, making up with enemies, coming to an acceptance of mortal life, developing a sense of serenity, feeling pride in accomplishment, and gaining a feeling of having done one's best (p.135)." The intent of the study was to examine what elderly people would do differently (such as spending more or less time) if they could relive their lives. There were 122 subjects who completed a questionnaire assessing the idea of life revision. For both males and for females, the pursuit of education and development of intellect was the most significant predictor. (DeGenova, 1992).

Although this study did not seek to enact active oral reminiscence or life review dynamics, the established theory base provides a context for new directions in research with the elderly. Learning about the things that people might do differently if they had the chance might be useful in interventions which focus on assisting the process of ego integration and the emergence of personal meaning in life (DeGenova, 1992).

Reminiscence is recognized as an adaptive coping process and is of positive value in stressful late life transitions. Fry (1991) studied two groups, each with a sample of seventy individuals. The methodology included structured interview and questionnaires which assessed the frequency of reminiscence activity and ratings of pleasantness associated with it. The measures used included measures of psychological well-being and meaning in life as predictor variables. Fry suggests that the results of the study have as their strongest application potential the possibility of identifying which elderly clients have the strongest potential for engaging frequently in reminiscence, finding it a pleasant experience, and deriving positive therapeutic outcome from the process of life review (Fry, 1991).

Haight (1991) performed a meta-analysis, examining nearly 100 articles on reminiscence and life review published in refereed journals over the last thirty years. Only seven articles report negative outcomes. Haight prescriptively concludes that the clinical use of reminiscence and life review with elderly clients should be encouraged and researchers should continue to define the variables that predict successful reminiscing. Butler's work in defining the parameters of life review is honored in Haight's article. Reminiscing is described as an umbrella which includes the more specific process of life review. The various types of life review: interpersonal, informative, and obsessive are identified. Many of the reported studies are intensive single case study designs, with methodology that is unique to the client, therapist, and environment. Haight suggests that developing a prescriptive methodology is a positive trend to encourage (Haight, 1991).

An important contribution made by Haight's meta-analysis of life review research is a series of box score summary tables which identify many of the studies' variables, subjects, and research questions (see Appendix A). The present study in life review is designed based on findings in Haight's meta-analysis (Haight, 1991).

Examples of anecdotal review of life review research include such summary statements as that of Fallot (1980) who determined that reminiscing served an adaptive function decreasing both shame and depression. Ego integrity was seen as "positively related" to life review by Taft and Nehrke (1990), while Bergland (1982) saw it as a "positive influence" on self-esteem. Ellison (1981) reported group life review as qualitatively "promoting of successful aging" and that the small groups were "most helpful."

In a recent study published in the *Journal of Consulting and Clinical Psychology*, Arean, et al. (1993) compared effects of problem-solving therapy, reminiscence therapy, or waiting-list control on 75 randomly assigned older adults diagnosed with major depressive disorder. At post-treatment, both treatment conditions produced significant reductions in depressive symptoms, compared with waiting list control group. Arean's study is, to date, the most methodologically rigorous treatment outcome evidence of effectiveness of the life review as applied to depression (Arean et al., 1993).

GROUP PSYCHOTHERAPY

According to Yalom's group dynamic approach (Yalom, 1985) personalities are the learned product of social interactions. The nature of these interactions, real or perceived, affects how persons develop and who they are. This perspective relies on persons as part of larger, holistic systems. Human behavior is learned through the process of socialization and interaction. Through interactions, people learn how to behave, think, and feel. Behavior is determined from within as well as by outer, environmental experience. Behavior is therefore learned or socialized interaction. The interpersonal relationships in the early family system and social environment of an individual, when distressed and/or dysfunctional, provide a socialization experience which fosters a pathological personality. People learn to behave in socially and psychologically healthy or adaptive manner or they are socialized to behave and process reality in unhealthy ways (Yalom, 1985).

Theory of Group Psychotherapy

Group counseling may act as a vehicle for helping people make changes in their attitudes, beliefs about themselves and others, and in their feelings. Groups are a social microcosm, offering support of other members and helping each member to realize that they are not alone in their struggles (Corey, 1992).

The two group approaches: the Structured Reminiscence and the Gestalt Life Review, generally based upon person centered (e.g., Carl Rogers) and group dynamic (e.g., Irvin Yalom) theoretical principles, share a number of fundamental similarities. All group counselors, regardless of theoretical orientation, are ethically bound to be responsible and responsive to their group members (Corey, 1992). They must communicate the role expectations, rights, and responsibilities to group members. Members must be informed of possible risks as well as benefits of potential life changes that may occur because of the group experience. Both models of group psychotherapy attempt to elicit change either cognitively, affectively, or behaviorally.

The person-centered therapy group aims to increase the congruence between members real and ideal self. It is the expectation that increased congruence leads to adjustment and emotional well being. People explore the full range of feelings, become increasingly open to new experiences, and gain in self-confidence in their own judgment. Group members have an opportunity to live in the present- developing openness, honesty, and spontaneity in a safe environment facilitated by the leader. The leader role also includes creating and maintaining a climate of trust, care, respect, and understanding. The qualities of genuineness, empathy, and unconditional positive regard are provided. The leader must trust the innate human directional tendency of the members to self-actualize and seek meaning.

Group psychotherapy process and dynamics. All groups go through a similar process of orientation and exploration. Members get to know each other and establish an atmosphere of trust. Commonly, members go through a transition stage of group development in which members may experience anxiety, resistance, and conflict. Trust normally gets tested in this phase. All effective therapy groups experience a "working" stage where group cohesion is further established. Group cohesion happens as a result of time spent together in a common experience, members' self-disclosure, feedback, and confrontation.

In group therapy, the foundational mechanisms for change rely on Yalom's therapeutic factors, (Yalom, 1985). The first is the instillation of hope, which occurs by members identification with other group members who overcome adversity. Next is universality, which develops when an individual's perception of uniqueness is dispelled. Information is imparted, which helps clients frame realistic expectations. The phenomena of altruism occurs by group members sharing experiences, insight, reassurance, and a sense of mutuality and caring.

Corrective recapitulation of the primary family group, within the systemic dynamics of the group, is another factor. Group participants may discover themselves engaging in familiar styles of interpersonal role dynamics upon encountering a multitude of transference-like relationships within the group. Members develop and practice socializing techniques, and try out new imitative behavior based on successful role models. Interpersonal learning happens in an atmosphere of group cohesiveness, with bonding, acceptance, affiliation, and respect between members. It is common for catharsis to occur. Members ventilate strong emotions, in an environment of permission and validation (Yalom, 1985).

Social support for older adults. Social support, available in the group psychotherapy format, appears to help distressed older adults in several ways (Janoff-Bulman & Wortman, 1977). By being available to talk with others about a painful event, distressing situation, or memory and the expression of depression, sadness, anger, loss, and other powerful emotions is permitted. Another factor which happens in situations of unconditional social support is the availability of others in order to assist in effective problem solving and reality checking. The weakness and helplessness often associated with ineffective coping and problem solving resources represent an unfortunate generalization. Powerlessness may be perceived as stigmatizing and have a negative effect on self-concept congruence, an effect which impedes adjustment and accommodation. It is relevant to note that while people can be genuinely helpless in preventing situations related to the stresses of aging, they can be powerfully proactive in coping with it.

Thompson (1985) noted that comparing one's situation with another's who is not perceived to be doing as well is another way of coping. Satisfaction with one's lot in life is somewhat dependent on whom one uses as a standard. Downward comparisons are likely in high threat situations. Comparing with those who are not doing as well can give a feeling of pride in one's own ability to handle a difficult situation. Self-efficacy may be enhanced or restored. This results in a feeling of being lucky and thankful that a worse possibility didn't occur. This phenomena may occur even though someone may have lost virtually everything (Thompson, 1985).

Another function that social support groups may serve is to provide people with information about how other's are reacting, perceiving, or remembering their experience (Wortman, 1983). This feedback can help facilitate more accurate and objective assessment about the distress and adjustment process they are enduring. Resocialization through group reminiscence is supported by work by Lowenthal and Marrazzo (1990).

A reminiscence group offers something quite different from one-to-one supportive relationships. The experience of social support may be facilitated within the unique process of the reminiscence group by maintaining some goals: by encouraging each person to speak during each meeting, by promoting relatedness and interaction among them, and by listening with sincere curiosity about their past experiences (Huber & Miller, 1984). Social support and interaction derived from group membership was reported to be related to life satisfaction in later life with older adults in retirement (Sagy & Antonovsky, 1990).

Issues of countertransference. The issue of a psychotherapist's own values and feelings, including countertransference issues, is an inevitable part of this discussion. The therapist must be neutral around the idea of death and dying. This neutrality is operationalized in an interesting way. There needs to be modeled the use of open, honest, and direct terminology to suggest and demonstrate that the therapist is comfortable discussing the subject. If the life review group members are to be free to express themselves, without self-censorship, the facilitators must ensure for them that they don't need to fear being perceived as insensitive, offensive or inappropriate. The coping mechanisms that are brought in to therapy need to be regarded with respect by the therapist (Knight, 1986).

The therapist must be neutral, as defined in this context, around issues of adjustment style, type of meaning sought as accommodation to this very stressful life crisis, their religious beliefs, and the pace each with which each older adult moves through the life review process. A therapist's own issues, feelings, and beliefs around aging, loss, and death are aroused. These issues need to be acknowledged, looked at, understood, and worked through to safeguard the therapeutic work done from any negative impact or affect-stifling therapist factors (Knight, 1986).

THE STRUCTURED REMINISCENCE LIFE REVIEW MODEL

Several consistently strong resources have contributed to the development of the structured reminiscence group model. Haight (1984; 1988; 1991) has continued to elaborate upon theory and conceptualization of life review work. The technical base of the structured model, that is, the use of focused stem prompts in generally pre-determined sequence has brought refinement to the process. Haight's contributions to the literature, such as the construction of a set of life review protocols, the definition of training needs, conceptual understanding for group leaders, and session outlines support program replication and ongoing research.

The American Association for Retired Persons provides a replicable, standardized format of the structured reminiscence life review group (AARP, 1994). Their life review model, which is thoroughly based upon person-centered dynamics, is used as a component of training for group facilitators nationwide. The AARP model is used to create an atmosphere where older adults can freely tell their stories- with the assurance that no interpretation, elaboration, or probing will occur. It is assumed that the telling of one's life story in a supportive and affiliative atmosphere is the goal in its entirety, much the same as Roger's (1957) necessary and sufficient conditions (e.g., empathy and warmth) were historically viewed as both the process and goal of person-centered therapy.

Structured Reminiscence Intervention

In the structured reminiscence intervention, techniques such as imagery are used to access memory. In this way, mental health professionals help clients recall past relationships and events, consider their meanings, and develop a sense of pride in accomplishment (Waters, 1995). According to Waters, the modality is non-directive with life reviewers being instructed to talk about whatever they wished.

Audiotaping of sessions and minimal directions by the interviewer permit non-intrusive dynamics and, as little as possible, influence the course of the reminiscence. Life reviewers in structured reminiscence may be assessed as to presence of depressive symptoms which include evidence of loss of self-esteem and expressed feelings of hopelessness and despair (McMahan & Rhudick, 1964).

For the older adult, examination and analysis of life history materials may be facilitated by working with the current life stage themes prompted by stem questions. Life stage themes and issues are relevant at their own level as well as serving as a derivative or pathway to earlier family and personal life history conflicts (Brok, 1992).

Art and music as components of structured life review. Burnside (1995) noted that art and music may be viable components of life review groups as adjunctive psychotherapeutic techniques for dealing with the feelings of loss and adjustment, inclusive of anticipatory and actual grieving. Art is presented as a potential vehicle for creating ritual and metaphor in this difficult process of life stage transition (Junge, 1985). This includes memories and events both good and bad wherein life review group members are asked to bring photos or momento-like objects to group meetings. Over the series of sessions, the members talks about the feelings brought up in the doing of the art and acknowledge the difficult but meaningful nature of the task.

Some structured reminiscence groups invite members to bring in markers, crayons and collage materials while at times directed by the therapist in specific theme areas. At other times, free drawing is encouraged. Artwork may center around typical issues of grieving, separation, and loss (Gilbert, 1977). Other uses of art include augmentation of memory recall by holding or looking at some treasured memory object as a between group session, individualized structured exercise.

Artwork in the life review group context may serve as a preventive intervention technique in grounding and preparing the members for actual losses. It may be instrumental in establishing a sense of ritual to aid in a successful transition through grief and adjustment associated with depression, helplessness, and despair. The very process of artwork may be a vehicle for reminiscence, life review, and may provide context for reaffirmation of intimacy and validation of feelings. This kind of acknowledgment can be crucial in the process of saying good-bye and going on (Junge, 1985).

Music can induce feelings, memories, ideas, and associations that can be points of projection into discussion of present or past concerns. The use of songs with distinctive lyrics can assist the older adult in remembering. It can open lines of communication between therapist and clients and between the group members themselves (Gilbert, 1977). The integral connection between religion and music can engender comfort and reassurance. The expression of feelings about impending separation and loss, of a loved spouse for example, is a crucial need for healthy adjustment.

Music therapy is effective in providing life reviewers with important means for support and tools for change (Bailey, 1984). The lyrics and tunes represent reminiscence, induce affective communication, effect cognitive stimulation, and develop group cohesion. Older adults experience feelings of isolation, depression, tension, loss, grief, and pain. Coping mechanisms that individuals use to deal with these emotions and concomitant changes are usually those called upon in their pasts (Bailey, 1984). Additionally, during the expressional process of music therapy, many conflicts, ambivalences, and issues of unfinished business may surface and possibly be reconciled.

Through the use of music, life reviewers gain access to problems, past or present unsatisfied needs or desires, and feelings of happiness or loneliness. Reminders of sad or happy times may provide insight into the way they are currently experiencing problems. This may also have the effect of distancing them from their immediate discomforts. Reminiscence may result in the discovery of unresolved issues. Also as a result of reminiscing, songs about relationships may bring up old business about anger, guilt, rejection, jealousy, and abandonment (Bailey, 1984).

Feelings of satisfaction and acceptance, suggestive of resolution, may be reflected in the song themes which commonly occur in the closure stage of this work. Songs link affect to thoughts, memories, events, and relationships. The messages diminish isolation, anxiety, and fear and can both provide inner support and help couples process changes, loss, and grief. Similar to the use of art, music too supports memory recall for evoking reminiscence when used as a between group session, individualized structured exercise.

GESTALT LIFE REVIEW MODEL

Life Review as a naturally emergent process of reminiscence in the elderly is presented by Crose (1990). Erikson's final developmental life stage/task of the struggle for ego integrity is noted as the ground where reminiscence may emerge for dealing with unfinished business. As a result of reminiscence, clients may move adaptively towards integration and resolution of problems. Crose reviews Gestalt therapy and its relevance and effectiveness in facilitating the resolution process in life review for older clients. Through the facilitated reminiscence clients may achieve closure on past events and relationships and live more fully in the present with increased ego integrity (Crose, 1990).

The Gestalt techniques cited in several case descriptions include, for example, the therapist's comments regarding incongruity between a client's words and displayed affect. This is objectively offered back to the client as an observation and query. This Gestalt process brings feelings out of the cognitive memory realm and into the affect of the here and now where resolution can possibly happen. The use of empty chair, re-enactment of memories, events, or dreams in sessions all work to move the client's reminiscence process into the present with activity and contact. In the case descriptions presented in this article, examples of the life review are provided, illustrating the value of the Gestalt approach for both female and male elderly (Crose, 1990).

Gestalt Therapy

Theoretical foundations of Gestalt. Corey (1985) states that goals give directions to a group and are determined by the theoretical premise of the specific therapeutic method. Gestalt is a form of existential therapy (Yontef & Simkin, 1989) based on the premise that individuals must find their own way in life and assume responsibility. The focus is on what the client experiences in the present moment and the blocks that the person must overcome to achieve full awareness in the here and now. The basic goal is to challenge participants to become aware of how they are avoiding responsibility for their awareness and to encourage them to look for internal, rather than external support.

A phenomenological approach. Perls' (1969) essential constructs of Gestalt are the "now" and the "how." "Now" covers all that exists and is the basis of awareness and "how" covers behavior and what is involved in the ongoing process. This is done by focusing on the obvious- on the surface of behavior. Gestalt concentrates on the client's movements, postures, language patterns, voice, gestures, and interactions with others. Gestalt therapists challenge group members to become aware and open to the here and now. Humans have an innate drive to growth, need fulfillment, and satisfaction. Accepting responsibility for one's integrated self is the expression of healthy personality.

As clients acquire present centered awareness and clearer perceptions of their blocks and conflicts, significant unfinished business emerges. Gestalt assumes that the way to become an autonomous person is to identify and deal with unfinished business from the past that interferes with present contact and functioning. By re-experiencing past conflicts and working through, clients expand their awareness and are able to integrate, thus becoming unified and whole (Corey, 1985).

Gestalt therapeutic approaches. The mechanism for change in gestalt is the integration of whole being through awareness and insight. By taking care of old business and assuming responsibility for all parts of self, people change. Group members learn to ask clearly and directly for what they want, learn how to deal with one another in the face of conflict, and learn to give support and energy to one another. By being able to challenge one another, to push beyond the boundaries of safety and what is known, a community based on trust is created. This process allows deep and meaningful work to happen. Members learn to make use of resources within the group rather than relying on the group leader.

The goals of gestalt group work are inclusive of integrating polarities within oneself, and achieving genuine contact with self and with others. Members practice defining their boundaries with clarity while becoming aware of what is sensed, felt, thought, fantasized, or done in the present. Insights are translated into action. Members demonstrate willingness to learn about themselves by engaging in creative experiments. Experience in learning to provide self-support instead of looking to others for this support happens in the group (Zinker, 1978).

Techniques used include language exercises, such as: "I" instead of "it" or "you," "won't" instead of "can't," "choose instead of should." Discrepancies and contradictions in messages from non-verbal language are brought to awareness and towards eventual integration. Examples are in movements, gestures, postures, voice, tone, pitch, or volume. Gestalt uses experiments with dialogues such as fantasy, splits, conflicts, and polarities. Other gestalt techniques include "making the rounds," use of empty chair, rehearsal of confrontational dialogues, role reversal, and dream work (Yontif & Simkin, 1989).

The gestalt group leader provides a climate in which clients can become more clearly focused on their changing awareness from moment to moment (Polster & Polster, 1973). Leaders help the clients make the transition from external to internal support by locating the impasse- or point at which clients get stuck by avoiding experiencing threatening feelings and attempt to manipulate others. Leaders challenge and frustrate group members by confronting the obvious. They create and suggest experiments (Zinker, 1978) and encourage members to assume responsibility. With Gestalt group therapy, the emphasis is upon the importance of helping an individual to greater contact, understanding, and integration of the "whole self" in the here and now. The therapist seeks to make the individual aware of who they are and what they are doing.

Application of Gestalt Model to Life Review Groups

Before the early 1960s, Perls' Gestalt model, as it was applied in group psychotherapy, looked very much like individual therapy using the "hot seat" in the middle of a group. Following an episode of interaction between the individual and the group leader, the other group members who had been silent observers would give feedback on how they were affected. In recent years the one-on-one model has been expanded to include a variety of awareness related group process exercises that engage creative exploration and emphasize group interpersonal dynamics (Yontef & Simkin, 1989).

Zinker (1978) pointed out that the expanded use of the group was certainly within Gestalt methodology. This included greater involvement of group members during an individual group member's period of the group leader's focus of attention. Also, the rigid adherence to all members participating in "making rounds" yields to what may be seen as a more individual choice (or *"chutzpa"*) based determinant of participation. Members may therefore retain the autonomy to choose the frequency, depth, and limits of disclosure and depth of processing.

The task of maintaining clear boundaries is shared by all, group leaders and members alike (Yontef & Simkin, 1989). In summary, it is an evolved Gestalt model that encourages both increased awareness and contact between group members, facilitates greater dynamism in the here and now, and is respectful of boundaries that is being applied to the present study's life review context.

Treatment strategies for Gestalt life review group process. The Gestalt life review group is qualitatively different from a typical group psychotherapy context. Since the group members are given specific structured stimulus prompts to reminisce as opposed to the emergence of therapeutic issues, it is the prompted reminiscence narrative which becomes "grist for the mill." At all times, the disclosing group member and other participants have the opportunity to be affected by and make contact with each other in the here and now. Group leaders may make suggestions from the many creative gestalt-related intervention options (e.g., empty chair, focusing) or facilitate interpersonal process awareness in the here and now (Zinker, 1978). The timing of interventions is based upon the clinical judgment of the group leaders based on perceived readiness of group members to process emergent issues toward possible resolution or closure (Greenberg, 1993).

Awareness exercises in Gestalt life review group. The use of some form of sensory integrative group exercise is a common component for structured reminiscence groups (AARP, 1994; Haight, 1995). A reminiscence group leader may choose from guided imagery, visualization, or progressive relaxation as all are accepted models of stress reducing exercises. In the Gestalt literature (Stevens, 1971), there are a number of sensory integrative exercises noted which, in addition to facilitating stress reduction, also support increased focus in the body, with enhanced awareness in the here and now. Adaptations of Stevens' work will be used in the Gestalt Life Review group treatment with these foci in mind.

SUMMARY

The review of related literature recognized the demographics and trends relevant to older adults. Issues of depression, grief, adjustment to loss and the impact on self-concept were also explored. The naturally occurring phenomena of reminiscence and its relation to adjustment concerns and the research into life review was discussed. Group psychotherapy with older adults, specifically structured reminiscence was visited. Finally, the theoretical and technical approaches of Gestalt group psychotherapy, orthodox and innovative, were examined and applied to a structured reminiscence model. The review of literature for the present study is concluded with a proposed synthesis and testing of a new model, the Gestalt life review group.

The Synthesis and Testing of a New Model in a Replicable Study

In a meta-analytic study of depression-related group work studies with older adult populations, Gorey and Cyrns (1991) noted that although outcomes were generally positive, they were for the most part not replicable and lacked empirical criteria. The same has been so in the study of life review groups (Haight, 1991; 1995). The present study seeks, in a psychotherapy analogue, to find a clear response regarding the comparable effects of two life review group psychotherapy treatments for older adults, the already existent Structured Reminiscence Life Review and the Gestalt Life Review, a synthesized "new model" on a selection of dependent variables. The a priori dependent variables in the present study are depression, belief in one's own helplessness, sense of congruence of self-concept, and achievement of ego integrity. The present study's methodology and manualization of treatment provides a model which may be applied and replicated in a variety of older adult populations and settings.

CHAPTER 3

Methodology

DISCUSSION OF SAMPLING PROCEDURE AND PARTICIPANT SELECTION

Accessing the Participant Pool

There was an initial mailing of 915 invitations to participate in the study. These were sent to retirees of Ball State University who still lived within a one hour driving distance from the campus. The coded, initial contact mailing included: 1) a letter of introduction and invitation to participate which included a statement of potential benefits and risks related to participation in the present study and a statement of confidentiality (Appendix A); 2) a pre-stamped response reply envelope for the return of the signed informed consent to treatment (Appendix B). The response letter provided the means by which prospective volunteers could indicate interest in participation in the study. The prospective participants also had the option of responding to the invitation by telephone.

Initial contact subjects were informed that their response, whether by letter or telephone, entered his or her name into a drawing for four prizes of $25 each. Their eligibility for the drawing was not contingent upon their agreement to participate further in the study but simply upon their "yes or no" reply. After an interval of two weeks, a second mailing of postcards were sent to the pool of retirees as a "follow-up" to the original invitations to participate (Appendix C).

Expanding the Participant Pool

A population sample of community living older adults, inclusive of persons of ethnic and racial diversity, was deemed desirable and the researcher determined to expand the circle of potential study participants. Thus, a second mailing of 221 announcements (Appendix E) was directed at all documented clergy in Delaware County with an invitation to inform those retired members of their respective congregations whom those clergy deemed potential participants of the study. Thirdly, a similar announcement (Appendix F) was placed in the May issue of *Prime Years*, a free magazine which is distributed to retired adults in Delaware County. The same protocols of informed consent and eligibility for the drawing were extended to these additional subjects.

Initial Response

Of the initial 915 invitations sent to Ball State retirees, there were 130 total responders. Fifty-five of the BSU retirees who responded to the initial announcement declined to participate for various reasons. Seventy-seven of the retirees agreed to participation in the study. Of the additional retirees contacted in the community, there were 44 responders, 33 of whom declined to participate for various reasons. Eleven of the community-based retirees agreed to participate. In total, 88 prospective participants were interviewed, screened, and pretested.

Screening Process

The continuing process of participant selection involved screening by means of structured telephone interviews (Appendix G). The telephone interviews were done by the researcher and several research assistants, and were conducted in a standardized format according to pre-determined protocols. A practice session was facilitated for the interviewers for rehearsal and role playing in order to maximize the consistency and standardization of the process.

In addition to obtaining demographic information, the interviewees were screened for cognitive impairment, such as any debilitating memory problems or confusion. Also, the IADL provided essential screening (and demographic) information, assuring that those interviewees, if selected, would be physically able to participate. At that time, those with severe cognitive impairment or physically debilitating restrictions were to be withdrawn from the available subject pool. Additionally, at that time there was an opportunity for the prospective subjects to ask further questions about the study.

Pre-testing Protocols

Upon completion of the telephone interview, all qualified candidates were mailed the complete research instrumentation package (Appendix H) which included first an informational/ instructional letter, then the SCL-90–R, and the combined pre-test dependent measures questionnaire for the present study: the Geriatric Depression Scale (30 items); the Irrational Beliefs Test (10 items); the Ego Integrity Scale (10 items); and the Life Satisfaction Index (10 items). Participants were asked to return all the completed forms in an enclosed pre-addressed, pre-stamped response envelope.

SCL-90–R as a Participant Screen at Pre-Testing

The SCL-90–R was used as a participant screening instrument at the onset of the present study, with specified upper limits cut-off T scores of 70 on several dimensions of current functioning: Depression, Anxiety and the General Severity Index (GSI). An examination of specific critical items (e.g., suicidality proneness) was done in the interest of screening out from further participation in the study of any persons even minimally at risk for whom the group life review process might have exacerbated any pre-existing psychological problems.

Prior to the onset of the life review treatment groups, a preliminary analysis of completed screening data revealed that the interviewed population sample was within the normal range of mental health-related current symptoms as reported in the SCL-90–R. The sample means (with standard deviation in parentheses) and percentile within the general adult (non-patient) population for the SCL-90–R variables of Depression, Anxiety, and the General Severity Index were 55.07 (9.71), 70%ile; 48.92 (10.58), 50%ile; and 54.39 (10.58), 68%ile respectively. The T-score range (+ or - 1 standard deviation) for normal adult non-patient is 40–60 (Derogatis, 1994).

Participant Screening Results

Eighty-eight completed research protocols were received. From the larger pool of 88 prospective participants, 23 subjects were eliminated from the available participant pool. Five resided in areas which were deemed by the interviewees as too distant from Muncie and withdrew themselves from further direct participation in the study. Of the 18 remaining persons, 12 were of insufficient age (under 65) for the study, 5, 4 withdrew for health-related reasons, and 2 were screened from the study for general concerns about mental health status. A final available participant pool numbering 65 was thereby derived.

The Stratified Randomization

It was determined at the outset of the study a stratified randomization should be a component of subject selection and assignment to treatment conditions. To that end, four subject groupings of the retired adult population were determined: 1) males who had professional or faculty careers (with educational level of masters or doctorate); 2) males who had support staff or clerical occupations (bachelor's degree or less); 3) female professional or faculty; and 4) female support staff.

A stratification of the 65 person available subject pool was developed. Random ordered lists were generated in the 4 stratification levels with 15 male professional, 10 male non-professional, 17 female professional and 23 female non-professional subjects in each category.

Assignment to Group and Treatment Condition

Thirty-six persons were selected and assigned to one of six groups (n = 6) with two groups for each treatment condition. These persons were notified by telephone and confirmed in writing of their eligibility for participation, the scheduling of groups, verification of location, etc. An additional alternate list of participants was randomly generated and contacted. If any of the 36 subjects became unable to participate or chose to withdraw from the study, the remaining alternate list would have been used to replace participants. All those persons who were selected as part of the WLC (no treatment) and persons on the alternate list were offered comparable group reminiscence experience to be provided by members of the life review group facilitation team to be scheduled at a later date.

The participant composition x stratification for each of the 6 groups (n=6) with 2 groups of each SRLR, GLR, and WLC treatment condition, was also determined by random generation. Table 2 describes the actual group composition following participant selection and assignment. Computed with an alpha of .05, the summary of

ANOVA on the stratification supported the validity of the randomization procedure with no significant differences in group composition, F (3,21) = 3.07, p =.411.

Table 2: Summary of Demographics: Stratification of Random Assignment

	Stratification Category			
Group	*Male/ Prof*	*Male/ Other*	*Fem/ Prof*	*Fem/ Other*
SRLR1	2	1	2	1
SRLR2	2	1	1	2
GLR1	1	2	1	2
GLR2	2	1	2	1
WLC1	2	1	1	2
WLC2	1	2	2	1
Total	10	8	9	9

Note. Male/ Prof = male professional retirees who had either masters or doctorate degrees; *Male/ Other* = male non-professional retirees who had either support or clerical occupations and bachelors degree or less; *Fem/ Prof* = female professional retirees who had either masters or doctorate degrees; *Fem/ Other* = female non-professional retirees who had either support or clerical occupations and bachelors degree or less; SRLR1 and SRLR2 = Structured Reminiscence Life Review; GLR1 and GLR2 = Gestalt Life Review; WLC1 and WLC2 = Wait List Control.

SCREENING MEASURES

Instrumental Activities of Daily Living (IADL)

As a component of the telephone interview, six questions derived from the OARS (Older Americans Resources and Services) Multidimensional Functional Assessment Questionnaire IADL measure provided further subject screening and demographic assessment in the present study. Items on the IADL scale are scored from 0 to 2, with 0 denoting the least functional. Scores may range from 0 to 12 with 12 indicating the most fully functional individual self-report. The IADL was developed as a research instrument by the Center for the Study of

Aging and Human Development (1978) and intended as a reliable and valid means of assessment of older individuals' instrumental and functional behavioral capabilities (Ernst & Ernst cited in Mangen & Peterson, 1984).

The OARS Instrumental Activities of Daily Living assesses the dimension of an older person's capacity for self-care, or activities of daily living. The IADL scale 2 week test-retest reliability is .71; p<.001. Inter-rater reliability for the scale is .74; p<.001 (Mangen & Peterson, 1982). Mangen and Peterson conclude that the ADL items included in the OARS have high discrimination power and that the questionnaire does measure the indicated dimensions of functioning and has strong construct and face validity.

Symptom Checklist-90–R

The Symptom Checklist-90–R (SCL-90–R) developed and revised by Derogatis (1994) is a 90 item self-report inventory. Each SCL-90–R item is rated on a 5 point Likert scale of reported distress level ranging from "Not at all" (0) to "Extremely" (4). SCL-90–R is an instrument which is designed to measure a subject's current, formative psychological symptom status and pattern and is not intended to measure trait personality factors. SCL-90–R has nine primary symptom dimensions, each empirically validated (Derogatis & Cleary, 1977, cited in Derogatis, 1994). It has been normed and shown to be reliable among psychiatric in-patients and normal adult non-patients, the latter being the relevant group for the present study (Derogatis, 1994).

The SCL-90–R has been used as an effective research instrument with older adults. Yesavage, Rose, and Spiegel (1982) used the instrument as a pre- and post-treatment measure in anxiety reduction treatment using relaxation training with the elderly. Also with older adults, three of the nine SCL-90–R symptom constructs (anxiety, depression, and interpersonal sensitivity) were used in a modified version with older adults as a measure of intimacy in older women's lives (Traupmann, Eckels, & Hatfield, 1982).

Although the dimensions of mental health related symptom functioning of the SCL-90–R were not used in the present study as a priori dependent variables, the obtained data were of value for subject screening purposes. The specific dimensions of interest for screening in the present study include the SCL- 90–R subscales for Depression, Anxiety, and the Global Severity Index (GSI). At a cut-off score of 70, critical items in these factors were examined. The GSI is the best single indicator of the current level or severity of any disorder noted on a subscale measure (Derogatis, 1994). The GSI combines information regarding the number of symptoms reported and the reported intensity of perceived distress.

Derogatis (1994) reports very good reliability of the subscales of the SCL-90–R in terms of internal consistency and 2 week test-retest reliability coefficients. The depression scale has a coefficient alpha of .90 and a test-retest r of .78, the anxiety scale has a coefficient alpha of .86 and a test-retest r of .80, the paranoid ideation scale has a coefficient alpha of .80 and a test-retest r of .84. In terms of construct and concurrent validity, SCL-90–R shows substantial correlation with other independent measures of the same constructs such as MMPI (Derogatis, Rickels & Rock, 1976, cited in Derogatis, 1994).

MEASURES OF DEPENDENT VARIABLES

Geriatric Depression Scale

The Geriatric Depression Scale (GDS) developed by Yesavage, et al. (1983) is a self-report scale indicating the presence of depression in older populations. The GDS is a 30 item questionnaire to which subjects respond by indicating yes or no to questions about depressive symptoms. It has been shown to be reliable among both normal and psychiatrically ill elderly (Norris, Gallagher, Wilson, & Winograd, 1987).

In the validity study (Norris et al., 1987) using the DSM-III (APA, 1987) diagnosis as the criterion, the GDS (at a cut-off score of 14) compared excellently with the Beck Depression Inventory (BDI) (Beck, Ward, Mendelson, et al., 1961) at a cut-off score of 17, for a correct hit rate of 84% for each of the instruments. The correlation between the two scales, the BDI and GDS, was .854 (p<.001; n = 67). Another measure of test validity, positive predictive value (PPV) was computed for the GDS in comparison to DSM criteria. At the cut-off score of 14, the PPV was 0.70 (Norris et al., 1987).

The GDS was selected over the BDI for the present study with the following rationale: Due to the multiple choice format of the BDI (Beck, 1961; 1978), the respondent must have sufficient concentration and short term memory skills to maintain enough information in working memory to respond to each item. The GDS uses a simpler yes or no format, requiring less cognitive effort for processing the questions, which may, according to Norris (1987) permit more accurate judgment of the appropriate response when testing older populations.

Life Satisfaction Index A

The Life Satisfaction Index A (LSIA), developed by Neugarten, Havighurst, and Tobin (1961) originally contained twenty statements, representative of the various ways in which older adult populations subjectively describe themselves on several dimensions of well being (Liang, 1984). The 20 item statements of the LSIA were each rated between strongly agree to strongly disagree on a 6 point Likert scale.

The LSIA views life satisfaction as multidimensional: zest versus apathy, resolution and fortitude, congruence between desired and achieved goals, positive self-concept, and mood tone (Neugarten et al., 1961). On the LSIA, an individual is assessed on a continuum of psychological well being, to the extent that he or she reports taking pleasure from whatever activities constitute his or her everyday life; regards that life as meaningful and accepts "that which life has been"; feels that he or she has succeeded in achieving major goals; holds a positive self concept; and maintains happy and optimistic attitudes or mood.

In the present study, a factor analyzed interpretation of the LSIA (Liang, 1984) was used. Based upon 10 of the original 20 LSIA statements, only the first-order factor Congruence subscale was deemed pertinent to the present study. Items with a factor loading of less than .45 have been eliminated from the scale's analysis. Liang's criteria (1984), such as face validity, construct validity, reliability, and correlated measurement errors, were used both to assign observed indicators to the latent factors and to determine which items to delete from the scored scale.

The LSIA model was evaluated using data from the 1974 National Council on Aging/Harris survey *(Myths and Realities of Aging in America)* which involved a nationwide sample of 2797 respondents. The shortened LSIA model of interpretation has been supported empirically and replicated consistently (Liang, 1984). Responses were examined using Pearson correlations and covariances. Computed with an alpha of .05, the loadings of the second order factors on congruence, varied from .669 to .998.

Irrational Beliefs Test

The Irrational Beliefs Test (IBT), developed by Jones (1977) was designed primarily as a research instrument to measure Albert Ellis' irrational belief system (Ellis, 1962) which relates the cause of emotional disturbance to the cognitive mediation of events by learned, irrational thoughts. Irrational beliefs self-handicap a person's ability to manage depression and other negative emotional states (Jones, 1977).

Although the IBT was developed to measure ten categories of irrational beliefs, only one subscale, Helplessness, is uniquely pertinent to the present study. The Helplessness subscale suggests that one's past history is an all important determiner of one's present behavior. It also suggests a belief that because something or someone once strongly affected a person's life, it should have the same effect indefinitely. The helplessness belief involves denial of responsibility for one's own behavior, makes it very difficult to meet current problems and stressors effectively, and makes it possible to abdicate responsibility for one's emotions, projecting the responsibility to other people or factors in the external environment (Jones, 1977). For purposes of the present study, a shortened version of the IBT, approved by Sweney (1996) was used with 10 items from the Helplessness subscale.

The IBT was normed on a population including older adults up to age 65. Responses to the IBT items are scored on a six point Likert scale ranging from strongly agree to strongly disagree. Reliability and validity for the IBT have been established satisfactorily (Jones, 1977). The Helplessness subscale, using Guilford's method (item-item correlations and homogeneity values) has a reliability coefficient of .726 with test-retest stability of .676. In terms of construct validity, Jones (1977) factor analyzed the IBT items and found the helplessness dimension to be one of ten clearly identifiable factors which accounted for 73.2% of the total variance.

Ego Integrity Scale

The Ego Integrity Scale (EIS), developed by Boylin, Gordon, and Nehrke (1976) is a measure of late life adjustment. The EIS was developed and operationalized on the basis of Erikson's (1963) ego integrity concept, the final developmental psychosocial life stage task of late adulthood, ages 65 years and over. It is the resolution of this developmental crisis that is of particular interest in the present study.

The EIS is a ten-item scale which reflects feelings and attitudes characteristic of the two alternate aspects of the final adult developmental stage: ego integrity or despair. Five of the items represent positive resolution of the stage (integrity) and five represent a negative resolution (despair). They are scored on a 6 point Likert scale from strongly agree to strongly disagree. As an unitary global index of the affect balance type, Ego Integrity - Despair is quantified on a 60 point continuum. The higher score is indicative of more differentiated ego integrity development.

Support for the validity and reliability of the Ego Integrity Scale was published by Walasky, Whitbourne, and Nehrke (1983). An inter-rater reliability coefficient of .73 was ascertained. Concurrent and construct validity of the EIS measure was suggested but further empirical study was reported by the authors as warranted (Walasky et al., 1983). The EIS was originally used with an all male sample (Boylin et al., 1976) and the question of generalization of Erikson's psychosocial conceptualization to women was part of a study of reminiscence and late life adjustment (Sherman & Peak, 1991). Sherman and Peak found no significant differences between the sexes on integrity scores of demographically matched samples.

POST-TESTING PROCEDURES

Following the eighth and final group meeting for each of the four life review groups (two in each condition: GLR 1 & GLR 2 and SRLR 1& 2) the battery of four dependent measures was repeated as post-testing. Participants in the SRLR, GLR, and WLC group conditions once again responded to the Geriatric Depression Scale, the Irrational Beliefs Test, the Ego Integrity Scale, and the Life Satisfaction Index. The SCL-90–R was used as a treatment exit screen.

ANALYSIS OF DATA

Data Processing

All operations pertaining to data encoding, processing, and subsequent statistical analysis for the present study were performed with the support of *SPSS Advanced Statistics™ 6.1 for the Macintosh* (SPSS Inc., 1994). Encoding of data was performed with the supervision of James A. Jones, Ph.D., Research Design Consultant at University Computing Services, Ball State University.

Statistical Analysis

The a priori statistical analysis was a repeated measures MANOVA of pre-and post treatment means to determine any significant interaction of treatment groups on dependent measures. This was to be followed by a series of univariate F tests on all variables with significant differences.

DESCRIPTIONS OF TREATMENT CONDITIONS

Site Selection and Details

The site selection of Lucina Hall on the Ball State University campus in Muncie, Indiana was based on the following criteria: The group room on this site used for the study was a well appointed "conference room" with comfortably upholstered furniture. This room was adequate in creating an attractive and secure environment, conducive to an atmosphere of safety and trust which the life review groups required. Lucina Hall's location was also quite familiar for the population sample in the present study and was easily accessible by persons with moderate physical disabilities. University Parking services agreed to furnish participants with temporary visitor's parking permits for the duration of the life review group study. The University Banquet and Catering services furnished coffee, tea, and cookies to the group member participants at each meeting.

Arrangements for the reserved use of the Lucina Hall facility were scheduled on Monday, Tuesday, Wednesday, and Thursday evenings on eight consecutive weeks. Research participants were notified of the confirmed life review group schedules immediately upon their selection and assignment to groups. The group participants were informed that any who required transportation to and from the Lucina Hall site, or who had pre-existing or emergent specific disability needs, would be assisted in such arrangements as were deemed necessary.

TREATMENT

Protocols for each of the 8 session group reminiscence treatments are described in detail in Appendix I, the *Facilitator's Manual for Reminiscence Groups*. The differences between the Structured Reminiscence Life Review group and the Gestalt Life Review group are presented in the manual. Outlines of session agendas and protocols are provided along with examples of appropriate sensory integrative group exercises, an established component of life review groups. Also included in the manual are a series of "homework" handouts with the stem prompts to reminiscence pertinent to each meeting of the 8 session series.

GROUP FACILITATION TEAM

In order to protect the present study from experimenter bias, the primary researcher, Steven Koffman, was not an active member of the reminiscence groups' facilitation team. The facilitation-service delivery team consisted of two Ph.D. level counseling psychologists, one male and one female. Both of these persons were experienced facilitators of group psychotherapy for whom the role of primary group leader became his or her responsibility. Each of the two psychologists led two of the life review groups, one each of the SRLR and the GLR condition.

Also on the team were two masters level counselors, both females, who had dual gerontological specialization and experience in life review group facilitation. One of these persons functioned as the process observer in all 32 one and one-half hour sessions. The second counselor's role was that of co-facilitator for, similarly, all 32 sessions. In addition to the training described in the following text section, all four of the team members engaged in regular feedback and debriefing sessions over the 8 week course of treatment. Telephone and email contact was maintained with the primary researcher, Steven Koffman, for similar purposes (e.g., decision making regarding emergent group dynamic concerns).

The Process Observer: Additional Data Collection and Recording

An in-group process observer fulfilled several functions in the present study. One of the two masters level life review group co-facilitators, trained in theory and methods for both the structured reminiscence and the Gestalt life review models, was present at all sessions of the two group treatments as a non-participating observer. This person's role as process observer was to monitor the individual group members' participation frequency and type of disclosure. The process observer also monitored the relative depth of subjects' affective experiencing. The process observer engaged in feedback and debriefing sessions with the group co-facilitators following each meeting. The feedback served to safeguard subjects' psychological well being by pointing out persons for whom any risk became either emergent or apparent.

The in-group process observer filled another valuable role in the present study. While attending to participants' disclosures and affective content, the facilitation of each session (e.g., type of responses, interventions suggested) was also monitored by the process observer. This assured that the primary group co-facilitators presented the actual life review treatment that had been promised in a technical manner consistent with the proscribed theoretical models. This substantive validity check, was augmented by recording of each session by audio tape. The process observer was also responsible for the transcriptions of all meetings of the experimental groups, coding of verbatim narrative to protect confidentiality, recording accurately the stem reminiscence prompts and members' response self-disclosures/ narratives, subsequent therapist interventions, and members' follow-up responses.

Training of Group Facilitators and Process Observer

The roles as life review group co-facilitators and in-group process observer required a "manualization" of training. The co-facilitators and the process observer had exposure to training modules which consisted of specific didactic learning and experiential exercises. The didactic component consisted of a series of readings and discussions. The readings were selected from the published work on group therapy and stages of group development and cohesion (Corey & Corey, 1988; Yalom, 1985), group facilitation with older adults (Toseland, 1990), and the life review literature. Selected readings encompassed the conceptual bases of reminiscence and life review goals and techniques (Haight, 1991; Lewis & Butler, 1974; Waters, 1990). Additional reading on theory, methods, and variations of Gestalt therapy and process with life review (Crose, 1990) was included in this training module.

The second didactic component consisted of videotapes of Gestalt (Perls, cited in Shostrum, 1964) and experiential therapy (Greenberg, 1994) in sessions which were observed and discussed by the team members in a training session. The AARP reminiscence and life review training program was also processed in the group. The training modules concluded with three sessions in which a triadic model of role play, role reversal, and observing was used. Trainees had opportunities to be in all roles with both SRLR and GLR experimental models which involved experiencing and focusing, as well as giving and receiving feedback. The experiences of the training sessions were processed by the group and seen variously as a useful experience for clarifying the treatment differential and as a positive interpersonal opportunity for the team to build trust and group cohesion.

PILOT VALIDITY GROUPS

Prior to the actual commencement of the 4 treatment groups (SRLR 1 & 2 and GLR 1 & 2) "role play" pilot groups were developed, facilitated, recorded, and assessed. The persons who role played older adults life reviewers in these pilot groups were volunteers solicited from the Ball State University community. The volunteers were a mix of graduate students and professional and support staff personnel at Ball State University. The pilot group gave informed consent to participate (Appendix J).

A sample group session for each treatment condition was enacted and videotaped. The two primary facilitators took turns in the two pilot group experiments; first as either the facilitator/ leader and alternately as an observer. A coin toss determined which of the two psychologists would lead either SRLR or GLR group. During the pilot group sessions, the designated observer and Steven Koffman watched the proceedings via monitor.

Although both pilot groups were provided with similar stem prompts and thematic derivation, the differential processing of emerging group member disclosure (e.g., reminiscence) was intended to be identifiably consistent with the two prescribed group treatments (SRLR and GLR) in both conceptual and technical aspects. Immediately following the pilot groups, the research team assembled for discussion, feedback, and debriefing sessions.

The videotapes of the role play pilot demonstration groups were submitted to an expert for review and feedback. The person designated as expert for this validity review was Mark Minear, Ph.D., a Postdoctoral Fellow in Geropsychology, qualified to act in the designated role as expert and consultant in the study of life review. The videotaped demonstrations met satisfactory criteria and the expert's feedback and suggestions for further clarification of the treatment differential were received and employed (Appendix K).

CHAPTER 4

Results

INTRODUCTION

This presentation of results will begin with a description of the results of the randomization. The hypotheses were examined using the 3 x 2 Multivariate Analysis of Variance statistical procedure as described in Chapter 3. Findings for each hypothesis will be presented individually. Following the analysis is a presentation of post hoc discovery.

RESULTS OF RANDOMIZATION ON SELECTED DEMOGRAPHIC VARIABLES

A series of univariate analyses of variance and a chi-square analysis were developed to assess the effectiveness of the stratified randomization on selected demographic variables of the participants in the study ($N = 36$).

Participant Age and Activities of Daily Living

Table 3, Participant Age and Activities of Daily Living x Group Assignment, provides the descriptive statistics on the two demographic variables, subject age and self report of activities of daily living competencies (e.g., vision, hearing, walking). Group means (with standard deviations in parentheses) for the age and ADL variables were 72.59 (5.42) and 11.08 (1.06) respectively.

The summary of ANOVA on ages of participants and ADL x group assignment, also indicated in Table 3, supports the validity of the stratified randomization process indicating no significant differences in group composition with an alpha level of .05.

Table 3: Means and Standard Deviations for Participant Age and Activities of Daily Living x Group Assignment

		Age	*ADL*
Group:	*n*	M (SD) *n*	M (SD)
SRLR1	6	72.67 (4.82) 6	11.83 (.37)
SRLR2	6	72.17 (6.89) 6	11.00 (.82)
GLR1	6	73.30 (3.64) 6	11.50 (.50)
GLR2	6	71.50 (7.26) 6	10.83 (1.07)
WLC1	6	73.83 (3.44) 6	11.00 (1.00)
WLC2	6	72.00 (5.03) 6	10.33 (1.49)
Total	36	72.59 (5.42) 36	11.08 (1.08)
Summary of ANOVA	df = 5 F = .13 n.s. *		df = 5 F = 1.52 n.s. *

Note. ADL = Activities of Daily Living, maximum score = 12. The higher the score, the fewer reported functional impairments. SRLR1 and SRLR2 = Structured Reminiscence Life Review; GLR1 and GLR2 = Gestalt Life Review; WLC1 and WLC2 = Wait List Control.

Participant Marital Status

Table 4, Marital Status x Group Assignment, provides the description of marital status categories (e.g., single, married, divorced, widowed) and frequency of participants who were assigned to each treatment condition. Due to the relatively small number of participants in each group (*n* = 6), participants in both groups of each treatment condition were combined (*n* = 12) for the chi square analysis. The Summary of Chi Squares, also reported in table 4, supports the validity of the stratified randomization on this demographic variable. With an alpha level of .05, it was determined that no significant association between marital status and group assignment was present, X^2 (6, N= 36) = 3.49, p = .75.

Table 4: Participant Marital Status x Group Assignment

		Marital Status			
Group:	n	single	married	divorced	widowed
SRLR1 & SRLR2	12	1	8	- -	3
GLR1 & GLR2	12	- -	7	2	3
WLC1 & WLC2	12	1	6	1	4
Total	36	2	21	3	10
Summary of Chi Square	$X^2 = 3.49$	df = 6	p = .75	n.s. *	

Note. SRLR1 and SRLR2 = Structured Reminiscence Life Review; GLR1 and GLR2 = Gestalt Life Review; WLC1 and WLC2 = Wait List Control.

RESULTS OF RANDOMIZATION ON PRE-TEST VARIABLES ACROSS GROUPS

Table 5, Pretesting, provides the descriptive statistics on the dependent variables at pretesting. Group grand means (with standard deviations in parentheses) for the Geriatric Depression Scale (GDS), Life Satisfaction Index A (LSIA), Irrational Beliefs Test (IBT), and the Ego Integrity Scale (EIS) variables at pretesting were 4.28 (3.84), 43.61 (8.60), 40.28 (7.91), and 40.0 (5.66) respectively.

Also shown in Table 5, a series of four univariate analyses of variance were developed to assess the effectiveness of the stratified randomization process of subject selection and assignment to groups based upon the pre-testing of the dependent variables as measured by the GDS, LSIA, IBT, and EIS. The ANOVA on the GDS, LSIA, and

EIS supported the validity of the stratified randomization process indicating no significant differences in group means with an alpha level of .05. There were no significant differences on the GDS, F (5,30) = .93, p = .475. There were no significant differences on the LSIA, F (5,30) = 1.26, p = .308. There were no significant differences on the EIS, F (5,30) = 1.93, p = .119.

The ANOVA on the IBT variable did detect a significant difference in pretest means in group SRLR2 (m = 46.0) and in group WLC1 (m = 46.5) in comparison with the other 4 groups (m = 37.29). The Tukey honestly significant comparison test provided challenge to the validity of the stratified randomization indicating the statistical significance of the between group difference . With an alpha level of .01, there were significant differences on the IBT, F (5,30) = 3.76, p= .009.

Table 5: Pretest Dependent Variables x Treatment

		GDS pre		LSIA pre
Group:	n	M (SD)	n	M (SD)
SRLR1	6	3.17 (3.76)	6	44.83 (6.37)
SRLR2	6	2.83 (2.64)	6	47.83 (7.99)
GLR1	5	5.33 (2.88)	5	43.17 (7.57)
GLR2	6	5.17 (4.17)	6	36.67 (8.91)
WLC1	6	6.33 (5.61)	6	43.0 (10.24)
WLC2	6	2.83 (3.31)	6	46.17 (9.04)
Total	35	4.28 (3.84)	35	43.61 (8.60)

df = 35 F = .93   df = 35 F = 1.2

p =.47   n.s. * p =.31   n.s. *

Note. GDS pre = Geriatric Depression Scale; *LSIA pre* = Life Satisfaction Index (Congruence); SRLR1 and SRLR2 = Structured Reminiscence Life Review; GLR1 and GLR2 = Gestalt Life Review; WLC1 and WLC2 = Wait List Control; * No two groups are significantly different at p < .05.

Table 5 *(continued)*: **Pretest Dependent Variables x Treatment**

		IBT pre		*EIS pre*
Group:	*n*	M (SD)	*n*	M (SD)
SRLR1	6	40.50 (4.32)	6	38.83 (6.08)
SRLR2	6	46.00 (6.63)**	6	43.83 (3.97)
GLR1	5	36.83 (7.17)	5	38.17 (5.67)
GLR2	6	32.83 (5.56)	6	35.67 (5.68)
WLC1	6	46.50 (7.23)**	6	41.00 (5.62)
WLC2	6	39.00 (8.46)	6	42.50 (4.64)
Total	35	40.28 (7.91)	36	40.00 (5.66)

df = 35 F = 3.76   df = 35 F = 1.93

p =.009   sig ** p = .12   n.s. *

Note. IBT pre = Irrational Beliefs Test (Helplessness); *EIS pre* = Ego Integrity Scale; SRLR1 and SRLR2 = Structured Reminiscence Life Review; GLR1 and GLR2 = Gestalt Life Review; WLC1 and WLC2 = Wait List Control; * No two groups are significantly different at $p < .05$; ** Denotes groups significantly different at $p < .01$.

DESCRIPTION OF THREATS TO RANDOMIZATION

Prior to the commencement of the 4 treatment groups, 2 individuals who had already been randomly selected and assigned to treatment conditions contacted the research team and asked, for personal reasons of convenience, if they could participate in the reminiscence study on some other night. Serendipitously, they were of the same stratification of the sample and could meet in each other's stead. In effect, one of the participants in the Monday night group traded places with another participant in the Wednesday night group.

In the 3rd week of treatment, a male participant in one of the groups announced his intention to voluntarily drop out from one of the GLR treatment groups. For reasons related to protecting the development of group cohesion and trust as well as the facilitation of group process in general (Yalom, 1988), it was determined not to replace him from the waiting list or alternate participant list. The groups lost no other members throughout the 8 week duration of treatment.

RESULTS OF THE MANOVA

A 3 x 2 (3 treatment conditions over 2 time periods) Repeated Measures Multivariate Analysis of Variance was performed upon the data. This overall test provided the means to explore whether or not differences were found over time, attributable to the treatment. Computed using an alpha level of .05, the MANOVA yielded a non-significant Omnibus F, $F (1,8) = .271$, $p = .54$. and therefore no evidence for a significant main effect.

As the 3 x 2 MANOVA analysis did not provide support for rejection of the null form of any of the 16 specific hypotheses of the study (H1a through H4d), the hypotheses were not further analyzed. Table 6, Pretest and Posttest Means and Standard Deviations of Four Dependent Variables, provides a summary of the descriptive statistics derived from the present study.

Table 6: Pretest—Post-test Means and Standard Deviations of 4 Dependent Variables

Source	n	Pretest M (SD)	n	Posttest M (SD)
GLR	11	GDS 5.82 (3.37)	11	GDS 5.18 (2.89)
		LSIA 38.27 (6.74)		LSIA 40.00 (6.00)
		IBT 35.27 (6.69)		IBT 35.82 (6.72)
		EIS 36.18 (5.17)		EIS 35.27 (5.10)
SRLR	12	GDS 4.33 (5.84)	12	GDS 3.33 (3.28)
		LSIA 43.75 (8.97)		LSIA 43.75 (7.07)
		IBT 40.50 (8.60)		IBT 41.90 (7.30)
		EIS 40.50 (6.01)		EIS 40.75 (8.00)
WLC	12	GDS 4.58 (4.56)	12	GDS 4.00 (4.52)
		LSIA 44.49 (9.64)		LSIA 42.33 (8.54)
		IBT 42.75 (7.85)		IBT 41.73 (6.84)
		EIS 41.75 (5.13)		EIS 37.60 (5.80)

Note. GDS = Geriatric Depression Scale; LSIA = Life Satisfaction Index (Congruence); IBT = Irrational Beliefs Test (Helplessness); EIS = Ego Integrity Scale; GLR = Gestalt Life Review; SRLR = Structured Reminiscence Life Review; WLC = Wait List Control.

POST HOC DISCOVERY

The Symptom Checklist-90–R Revisited

As described previously in Chapter 3, the SCL-90–R (DeRogatis, 1994) is an instrument designed to measure a subject's current symptom report status. A pattern emerged in the post hoc analysis of the SCL-90–R data. Participants in the Gestalt Life Review groups (GLR) showed statistically significant improvement at the time of post-testing on the SCL-90–R state constructs of Somatization, Positive Symptom Distress Index, Hostility, Interpersonal Sensitivity, and Depression. This contrasts distinctly from the participants in the SRLR and WLC treatment conditions where changes on these variables was not found. Descriptions of those 5 SCL-90–R dimensions follows. Following the in-text description of the SCL-90–R results is Table 7 which is a summary of the descriptive statistics. (see Appendix L).

Somatization. The Somatization dimension, as defined by it's use in the SCL-90–R (DeRogatis, 1977; 1994), " . . . reflects distress arising from perceptions of bodily dysfunction. Complaints focus on cardiovascular, gastrointestinal, respiratory systems. Reports of pain, general discomfort, and somatic anxiousness are also components of somatization (p.9).''

Computed using an alpha level of .05, the ANOVA showed a differential decrease approaching statistical significance on the SCL-90–R Somatization variable between the GLR treatment group versus the SRLR treatment and WLC no treatment groups, $F(1,2) = 2.88$, $p = .070$. Post treatment means (and standard deviation) compared to pre treatment were 57.82 (7.73), 55.50 (9.36), and 52.93 (10.73) versus 49.91 (11.39), 53.92 (9.13), and 52.47 (9.23) respectively.

Positive Symptom Distress Index. The Positive Symptom Distress Index, as defined by its use in the SCL-90–R (DeRogatis, 1994), is a "measure of symptom intensity as a function of participant response style- that is to say it reflects the process of augmenting or minimizing reports of symptomatic distress."

Computed using an alpha of .05, the ANOVA showed statistically significant differential decrease on the SCL-90–R Positive Symptom Distress Index variable in the GLR treatment group versus the SRLR and WLC groups, $F(1,2) = 3.61$, $p = .038$. Pre-treatment means (and standard deviation) compared to post-treatment were 60.27 (8.37), 53.67 (8.80), and 50.53 (10.47) versus 53.82 (7.37), 53.58 (8.49), and 51.13 (8.84) respectively.

Hostility. The Hostility dimension, as defined by its use in the SCL-90–R (DeRogatis, 1994), reflects " . . . thoughts, feelings, or actions characteristic of anger . . . and the expression of aggression, irritability, rage, and resentment (p.10)."

Computed using an alpha level of .05, the ANOVA showed statistically significant differential decrease on the SCL-90–R Hostility variable between the GLR treatment group versus the SRLR treatment and WLC no treatment groups, $F(1,2) = 3.645$, $p = .036$. Pre-treatment means (and standard deviation) compared to post-treatment were 50.09 (8.48), 47.00 (6.65), and 47.80 (8.36) versus 45.45 (6.80), 49.67 (5.85), and 45.93 (7.01) respectively.

Interpersonal Sensitivity. The Interpersonal Sensitivity dimension, as defined by its use in the SCL-90–R (DeRogatis, 1994), focuses on "feelings of inadequacy and inferiority, particularly in comparison with other people (p.10)." Included in this construct is an index of self-doubt and marked discomfort in social interactions.

Computed using an alpha of .05, the ANOVA showed statistically significant differential decreases on the SCL-90–R Interpersonal Sensitivity variable in the GLR treatment group versus the SRLR and WLC groups, F (1,2) = 4.35, p = .021. Pre-treatment means (and standard deviation) compared to post-treatment were 56.64 (6.98), 52.33 (10.29), and 49.33 (9.39) versus 50.82 (7.00), 53.50 (8.89), and 50.73 (7.95) respectively.

Depression. The Depression dimension, as defined by its use in the SCL-90–R (DeRogatis, 1994), reflects several of the DSM-IV criteria for a diagnosis of depression (APA, 1994). Included in the SCL-90–R depression construct are self-reported loss of pleasure, low energy, suicidal ideation, loneliness, worrying and hopelessness.

Computed using an alpha level of .05, the ANOVA showed statistically significant differential decrease on the SCL-90–R Depression variable between the GLR treatment group versus the SRLR treatment and WLC, F (1,2) = 4.57, p = .017. Pre-treatment means (and standard deviation) compared to post-treatment were 58.09 (4.89), 55.33 (7.51), and 52.47 (9.53) versus 51.82 (6.40), 55.17 (7.12), and 53.20 (7.30) respectively.

Table 7: Summary of Post Hoc SCL-90–R Variables: Means and Standard Deviations

	PSDI	*HOS*	*SOM*
Group:	M (SD)	M (SD)	M (SD)
GLR			
pre	60.27 (8.37)	50.09 (8.48)	57.82 (7.73)
post	53.82 (7.37) *	45.45 (6.80) *	49.91 (11.39)
SRLR			
pre	53.67 (8.80)	47.00 (6.65)	55.50 (9.36)
post	53.58 (8.49)	49.67 (5.85)	53.92 (9.13)
WLC			
pre	50.53 (10.47)	47.80 (8.36)	52.93 (10.73)
post	51.13 (8.84)	45.93 (7.01)	52.47 (9.23)
	$F(1,2) = 3.61$,	$F(1,2) = 3.645$,	$F(1,2) = 2.88$,
	$p = .038$ *	$p = .036$ *	$p = .070$ n.s.

Note. *PSDI* = Positive Symptom Distress Index; *HOS* = Hostility;
SOM = Somatization; SRLR = Structured Reminiscence Life Review;
GLR = Gestalt Life Review; WLC = Wait List Control;
* GLR groups are significantly different at $p < .05$.

Table 7 *(continued)*: **Summary of Post Hoc SCL-90–R Variables: Means and Standard Deviations**

	IS	*DEP*
Group:	M (SD)	M (SD)
GLR		
pre	56.64 (6.98)	58.09 (4.89)
post	50.82 (7.00)*	51.82 (6.40) *
SRLR		
pre	52.33 (10.29)	55.33 (7.51)
post	53.50 (8.89)	55.17 (7.12)
WLC		
pre	49.33 (9.39)	52.47 (9.53)
post	50.73 (7.95)	53.20 (7.30)
	$F(1,2) = 4.35,$	$F(1,2) = 4.57,$
	$p = .021$ *	$p = .017$ *

Note. IS = Interpersonal Sensitivity; *DEP* = Depression; SRLR = Structured Reminiscence Life Review; GLR = Gestalt Life Review; WLC = Wait List Control; * GLR groups are significantly different at $p < .05$.

CHAPTER 5

Discussion

INTRODUCTION

The sampling procedures accessed a population of non-patient volunteers for participation in the study of comparative group life review programs. They were a group for whom any marked psychopathology or elevated adjustment distress appeared absent at the outset. Nor was there any statistically significant change noted on the study's dependent variables at post-testing. The post hoc discovery on the SCL 90–R variables is interesting, but what conclusions can be drawn? In terms of external validity, what inferences may be relevantly applied or generalized to the larger population of retired older adults-at-large? What cautions are rightly taken in making such generalizations?

In response to these questions, several distinct areas are addressed. The population sample is examined in light of what demographic parameters were predicted by the literature review. Conceptualization of possible self-selection dynamics by participants is explored. The potential contributions of the study to the literature are reviewed, particularly the manualized intervention, development of the Gestalt life review group, and the replicable research model. The outcome of the study provides some reflection on adjustment concerns of older adults as described in the review of literature and related research. Some conclusions and inferences on ego integrity, self-concept, helplessness, loss, bereavement, and depression are made.

The study's similarity to comparative psychotherapy treatment is acknowledged. The findings on the SCL 90–R variables are reviewed and several follow up studies are suggested. General practice and research applications of the replicable model are offered. Other exploratory approaches to the data drawn from the present study of life review, such as qualitative or thematic analyses are provided.

THE POPULATION SAMPLE

The participants in the present study did not demonstrate the frequency of adjustment-related problems and distress, such as depression, as are found in the general population (Ham & Meyers, 1993). Scores on SCL 90–R variables were well within a non-pathological mid-range for adult non-patient norms (Derogatis, 1994). All participants were well within the normal range of positive functioning on both short and long term memory criterion, as well as orientation to person, place, time, and situation. Participants' IADL data were consistent with predicted frequency in the general population (AARP, 1995). Butler and Lewis (1974) noted that 70% of older adults lived with either their spouses or other relatives and had what was deemed sufficient social support. This is contrasted with the present study, where 89% of the participants lived with either spouse or family.

In summary, this sample of older adults failed to demonstrate the predicted frequency of adjustment and aging-related concerns (e.g., issues of loss, depression, confusion) as anticipated by the literature review (National Institute on Aging et al., 1994; Slater, 1995). Self-selection criteria may have influenced the degree to which individual participants volunteered for the study, and provides an explanation why the sample failed to be more representative of the general population.

Self-selection of participants. Based upon self-reports of those respondents to the original invitation to participate who chose not to be included in the available subject pool, several emergent themes were suggested. Issues included: chronic hospitalization for medical concerns for self or spouse, despair and loneliness over the death of a spouse, self-reported descriptions of symptoms of depression such as despair and helplessness, loss of motivation or interest in pleasurable activities. Some potential subjects refused participation in agitated and emphatic tones, "No and don't bother me again" while the tone of others seemed rather sad, "I'm so sorry that I am unable to participate." Another theme was of regret and grieving by widowed spouses, "He could have told you of horse and buggy days . . . farming with horses . . . probably more . . . his first car in 1929 . . . I'm so sorry."

Some of the original respondents declared themselves to be "too busy" with activities they had already committed their time and energies to, or others were admittedly in a kind of denial, "whistling past the graveyard" and didn't want to be associated with other "old fogies jawing about old times..no point to it." Others were self-described as active travelers, "I'm in and out of town too much to be reliable." One female respondent who declined participation in the study, countered with an invitation to accompany her on a weekend with her on her Harley-Davidson, "to find out what some retired people are really like."

Continuity theory. In consideration of the actual demographics of the participant pool and the self-screening examples provided, the Continuity theory of older adult development (Atchley, 1989) provides a foundation for conceptualizing this process. Continuity theory assumes that in making adaptive choices, older adults "attempt to preserve and maintain existing social patterns" (p. 35) by engaging familiar cognitive, behavioral, and affective schemas.

Continuity theory offers an explanation for the self-selection in the present study suggesting that prospective participants had applied their accustomed response patterns to the stimulus of an invitation to engage in the social and research activity of joining a reminiscence group. It is possible that those who chose to remain in the subject pool were able to recognize an opportunity to further an already familiar type of experience. One could further hypothesize that subject self-efficacy and social skills concerns were not taxed by the potential risk-taking implicit in participation in the reminiscence group study. Finally, it could be hypothesized that one could predict willingness to voluntarily participate in the present study by an absence of depression-related symptoms.

THE MANUALIZED INTERVENTION PROTOCOLS

Previous literature provided generally flexible format and guidelines for facilitating a structured reminiscence group, sufficient for practice application (Haight, 1984; Tobin, 1991; Toseland, 1995). The manualized protocols developed for use in the present study (Appendix I), which specifically describe content and process guidelines for an 8 session life review group psychotherapy intervention relied upon materials synthesized from the literature (Haight & AARP, 1994; Haight, Coleman & Lord, 1995; Peachy, 1992; Romaniuk &

Romaniuk, 1981). Additional sources were of value in designing the GLR treatment protocols (Crose, 1990; Gendlin, 1996; Stevens, 1971; Yontif & Simkin, 1989; Zinker, 1978), specifically in regards to integrating Gestalt conceptualization and techniques with group reminiscence stimuli.

In summary, the manualized intervention adds to the literature in two distinct manners. First, as a result of the study there now exists general group facilitation protocols for the Gestalt life review, the GLR. Second, there now exists a replicable format for further study of life review process. This provides a unique basis and support for ongoing research to increase the empirical knowledge base around reminiscence phenomena. As Moody (1988) noted, life review appeared to have potential adaptational significance on mental health variables. Empirical verification of its value on life adjustment for older adult populations is important in ethical and timely treatment planning.

ADJUSTMENT CONCERNS OF OLDER ADULTS

Ego integrity. Taft and Nehrke (1990) determined that life review was a probable mediator of ego integrity. The present study's results neither support nor disconfirm their findings. In the sample accessed, ego integrity was already well established at pre-testing. Carlson (1984) found a positive correlation between ego integrity development and reminiscing in general. The self-selection discussed in continuity theory (Atchley, 1989) provides a tentative explanation for this phenomena. The present study did not provide support for structured reminiscence in terms of resolution of Erikson's ego integrity task, a conclusion that Holzberg (1984) had suggested.

Self-concept and life satisfaction. Lewis (1971) found that older adults who expressed reminiscence behavior and demonstrated consistency of past and present self-concept were likely to manage unexpected life stressors effectively, an indicator of adaptiveness. Perhaps another determinant of self-selection or self-screening, strong congruence of self-concept seemed evident in nearly all the participants, as suggested by the pre and post testing on the Life Satisfaction Index (LSIA). The present study failed to demonstrate support for Haight's (1984; 1988) findings that structured life review would cause significant increase on LSIA scores. Perotta and Meacham (1982), on the other hand, concluded that it was questionable whether reminiscence was effective as a short term intervention on self-concept and depression.

Loss and bereavement. As Berlatsky (1962) had theorized and Carlson (1984) had determined, reminiscence not only supported mourning but facilitated movement from depressive signs of hopelessness in the direction of normal adjustment to losses. In reference to Wolfelt's (1988) distinctions between depression and grief, several dimensions were elucidated and noticeably impacted for some of the group members.

The experience of one participant provides an anecdotal illustration of movement from depressive symptoms towards expression of normal grief over the course of treatment, a marker of positive adjustment. A participant initially presented with memories of herself as being a poor parent while also an isolated and lonely spouse. At first, she was uninterested in support yet over the life span of her group she moved towards a responsiveness to comfort and support offered by others. Where she had been previously irritable and complaining, the movement was toward acceptance and open expression of anger. Where she had generalized feelings of guilt, she became more specific in terms of her guilt regarding defined losses.

Depression. Arean et al. (1993) had studied reminiscence therapy on older adults with a diagnosis of major depressive disorder and found that the treatment produced statistically significant reductions in symptoms. The present study differs in that the available subject pool of non-patient volunteers from which the sample was drawn were demonstrably free of diagnosable depression or other affective disorders.

Other than the SCL 90–R post hoc criteria where the GLR groups improved, there was no significant change in any of the treatment groups on depression. The SCL 90–R findings of the present study were consistent with the findings of Fallot (1980) who found that reminiscence served an adaptive function of decreasing depression. The present study's post hoc results offer some support for a study by Scates, Randolph, Gutch, and Knight (1986) who suggested that reminiscence treatment, although statistically non-significant, might have an impact on state-related affective disorders.

In summary, the measures of late life adjustment used in the present study failed to detect any changes in depression, belief in one's helplessness, self-concept congruence, and development of ego integrity in the participant sample. The dependent variables measured were apparently stable psychological dimensions, behaving more as though enduring personality traits, unchanged as a result of the 8 week life review group treatments.

DIFFERENTIAL TREATMENT EFFECTS

There was no evidence of differential treatment effects by either the SRLR or the GLR treatments. Null effect results such as those demonstrated in the present study might have been predicted by Luborsky, Singer, and Luborsky (1975) in the "Dodo Bird Verdict." Luborsky et al. had criticized psychotherapy research which sought to compare effects of different treatments, and concluded that specific treatments have less bearing on outcome effects than other variables (e.g., therapeutic relationship factors).

Beutler (1991) offered an opinion in response to Luborsky et al. which supports an investigation into comparative psychotherapy treatment efficacy, such as was done in this study. Beutler suggested that coordinated studies that follow up a model of prescriptive treatment selection enable clinicians to specify and prioritize client and treatment variables which might likely predict positive outcome.

There exists another possible explanation for the lack of any statistically significant treatment effect on the study's dependent variables. Perhaps the standardized instruments selected to measure the designated a priori dimensions of adjustment in older adults were not the right choice. It could be that the SCL-90–R would have been a better choice for the MANOVA.

THE POST HOC DISCOVERY

In any post hoc exploration of data, conclusions drawn must be cautiously offered. Controlling for experiment-wise error, possibility of type I or type II error, or assuming the possibility of randomness are all appropriate cautionary guidelines (Kerlinger, 1986; Stevens, 1990).

The discovery of the potentially significant interaction of the GLR treatment on the SCL 90–R state variables on Positive Symptom Distress, Hostility, Interpersonal Sensitivity, and Depression is an interesting finding. These results suggest a follow-up replication study focused within a population of older adults with any of those presenting psychological issues. It is intriguing to suppose that a Gestalt group psychotherapy model, combined with established structured reminiscence group protocols might predict effective treatment outcomes on those SCL 90–R variables and may imply a genuine resource for distressed older adult populations.

Suggested follow-up. A replication of the present study, adhering to the methodology and the manualization of treatment in the present study seems justified. Pre- and post-testing on the 5 SCL 90–R state variables instead of the present study's dependent variable is appropriate. Results derived from such an analysis could have the potential for directing prescriptive treatment in future clinical applications for older adult populations with presenting issues related to Positive Symptom Distress, Hostility, Interpersonal Sensitivity, and Depression. Institutionalized or nursing home residing older adults may more likely provide a population with these concerns.

PRACTICE AND RESEARCH APPLICATIONS OF THE REPLICABLE MODEL

The participants in the SRLR, GLR, and WLC groups showed by their screening, pre- and post-testing assessment to be relatively non-distressed and within the normal non-patient adult range of psychological functioning. This may be considered baseline data, of value in comparing replications of the present study with treatment effects in other, more distressed older adult populations. Limitations, as noted in Chapter 1, acknowledged a number of older adult populations which were beyond the scope of the study and might reasonably be populations of focus in future replications of the structured reminiscence life review study. Further study is suggested for populations of:

1. Older adult persons for whom a primary DSM-IV diagnosis is major depression, anxiety, other mood or thought disorders.
2. Institutionalized elderly, who are unable to perform a minimum of IADL functions.
3. Older adults with severe memory impairment and/or confusion.
4. Older adults of comparative age cohort membership, disability, gender, or marital status or representative of diversity populations.
5. Differences between institutionalized (nursing homes, hospitals) and non-institutionalized older adults.

CONCLUDING REMARKS

Gorey and Cyrns (1991) noted that although group psychotherapy with older adult populations had outcomes which were generally positive, they had lacked empirical criteria for evaluation. Critiques of group life review research have consistently noted the qualitative tone regarding outcome analysis (Haight, 1991). Previous reviews have suggested that group life review seemed (a) "adaptive and seemed to decreased shame" (Fallot, 1980), (b) "positively related to ego integrity" (Taft & Nehrke,1990), (c) "a positive influence on self-esteem" (Bergland, 1982), and (d) "most helpful in promoting of successful aging" (Ellison 1981).

In conclusion, the group participants indicated that they had felt positive about their reminiscence group experience. In the final meeting of one of the GLR groups, there was a dialogue between group members to the effect that, although they had not perceived themselves as dramatically changed due to the life review group experience, they were very aware that both the social interactions and the chance to have listened to each other's intimate life stories were precious to them. A few participants said that they felt less alone in their struggles and were grateful for the new frame of reference (Yalom, 1985). Some talked about getting together again in the future since new foundations of social support and friendship had been made (Haight, 1994; Tobin, 1991; Toseland, 1995). The experience of the life review had been meaningful and rewarding for them . . . maybe even something interesting to reminisce about.

Appendices A - L

Life Review Meta-Analyses (adapted from Haight, 1991)

APPENDIX A

Summary of Life Review Research

Study	Subjects	Measures	Outcomes
Carlson, C.M. (1984).	* N= 8 * Community Resid.	*Correlational study * Ego Integrity Scale :: reminiscing *One-hour interview	* Positive correl: * Reminiscing :: * adaptive funct :: * ego integrity.
Coleman, P.C. (1974).	* N=48 (F, M) * Age range = 69-92 Mean age = 80 * living alone in sheltered housing. * 6 mtgs (1.5-2 yrs)	* Qualitative/ Descriptive Study: * Structured Intview to "investigate function of remin". * used audiotape	* Life review was found to be of more significant benefit than simple reminiscing.
David, D. (1990).	*N= 43 (F, M) *Age range =68- *Retirement commun.	* Qualitative Study: * Interview format: * Life Satisfaction:: * Self-esteem	* Social context = important variable that shapes the relationship bet reminiscence and adaptation old age.
Fallot, R.D. (1980).	*N= 36 (all Females) *Age range=46-85	* 1 hr of reminiscing * self report of Mood * Mood Adjective Checklist	* Reminiscing can serve as adaptive function: * decreased both __depress & shame
Haight, B.K. (1988).	* N= 60 * homebound elderly * 6 week program	* "therapeutic role" of structured LR * LSIA * Self-Rat. Dep. Sc. * Affect Balance Sc. * ADL	* Signif Improve in: * Life satisfaction * Psych Well-Being * Life review did not produce depression in the exper group.
Haight, B.K. (1984).	*N= 12 *Age=60 and over. *6 wk intervention	* Exp & control grps *Therapeutic role:LR *LR Exper. Form	* Increase (NS) in: * life satisfaction in LR participants
Lewis, C.N. (1971).	*N= 24 (all Males) *Age=65 and older. * 1 hr conversation	*Correlational study: * Incr. Consistency of self-concept:: * Stress as IV	* Signif increase in past to present s-c * Suggest possibility of reminiscence as a defense mechanism.

McMahon,A.W & Rhudick,P.J. (1964).	* N= 25
	* Age 75-90
	* Veteran population
	  * depressed
	  * non-depressed
		* Correlational Study
		  *intellectual vars.
		  *self-esteem maint.
		*1 hour interview
		* social interchange
			* Non-dep indiv rem.
			  more than dep.
			* higher self-esteem

Romaniuk, M., & Romaniuk, J. (1981).	*N=91	* Self-report survey
		  of reminiscence
			* Relationship bet
			  remin :: adjustment
			  may the due to
			  measuring it inter
			  personaly vs intra-
			  personally.

Taft, L.B., & Nehrke, M.F. (1990).	* N=30. *Mean Age=84.13.	* Correlational Study * use of life review:: * remin frequency:: * ego integrity	*Use of life review * positively related to ego integrity * Frequency = no rel

Vickers, W.D. (1983).	* N=9 (all Males)
	* Mean age = 81
	* in & out patients at
	  a VA hospital.
	* Structured Remin.
		* Qualitative study
		*4 contacts @ S
		* Initial meeting
		* Audiotape history
		  (15 min. struct)
		* transcription
			*"suggests it was
			  worthwhile exper."
			**expressed interest
			  in further rem with
			  their families."

Bergland, C. (1982).	* N=14
	* 2 groups:
	  * grp 1: (7 women)
	  * longterm nursing
	  home.
	  * grp 2: (7 M & F)
	  * private shortterm
	  psychiatric hosp.
	* 1.5 hrs @ wk x 4
	mo
		* Pre and post LR tx
		  projective assess:
		  * Art work
		  * "Life lines"
			* Life review: seen as
			  "positive influence
			  on increased self-
			  esteem"
			* Research need:
			  further study with
			  increased numbers.

Dietsche, L.M. (1979)	* N=10
	* Mean Age = 73.2
	* Ambulatory day
	  care center pop:
	  * w/ known health
	  problems
	* 40-60 min @ wk x
	15 weeks.
		*Qualitative study
		* Specific, agreed
		  upon topic for each
		  session
		* LR through group
		  reminiscences
			* Shared life review
			  helped participants
			  * "to restructure &
			  gain an identity"
			  * incr in confidence
			  * incr self-respect

Ellison, K.B. (1981)	* N=5, Age =70-96
	* Nursing home resid
	  w/ no psychopath.
	* 1 hr @ wk x 8 wk
		*Qualitative study	* LR "promote
			  successful aging".
			* small group setting
			  most helpful.

Goldwasser, A.N, Auerbach, S.M, & Harkins, S.W. (1987).	* Demented nursing home residents. *.5 hr, 2x/wk x 5wks * Rem, No tx, cont grp (@ N=9) * 6 wks followup test	* Mini-Mental State * BDI * Behavioral effects: * ADL	* Rem grp higher on measures of cog & affective functon. * ADL-no change * Depression incr. 6 weeks later.
Holzberg, C.S. (1984).	* N=25 * Age=70-95. * residents integrated geriatric facility * Memoirs group * 1x @ wk x 11 mos.	* Qualitative study * Anthropologist interviews and audiotapes * Preserve history of immigration exper.	* "suggest" resolution of Ego Integrity * Memoir enabled * Validatrion as: * life offering * self validity exper
Ingersoll, B., & Goodman, L. (1980).	* N=10 * Age=69-98. * Institutional pop. Jewish Residents. * Group intervention 6 sessions.	* Qualitative study * Goal: Facilitate reminiscing among institutional elders * No measure.	* Leaders & members: "positive experience" * Increased: * Feelings selfworth * Social utilization. * Enhanced identity
Lappe, J.M. (1987).	* N=83 (8 grps) * Mean Age=82.6 yrs. * Pop. from 4 private longterm care * 4 @ Rem. vs CE * 10 wk intervention	* Reminiscence grps :: current events control grp * Rosenberg SE Scale	* 2 way ANOVA * Remin. increased self-esteem :: disc of current events.
Matteson M.A, & Munsat,E.M. (1982)	* N=7 (Age 75-85) * Intermediate Care facility * 6: mild to severe depressed * 8 sessions @ .5 hr * 2 grp facilitators	* Group reminiscing therapy with depressed elderly clients	* Goals partially met. * Some incr in social activity (NS). * Collaborative leadership model for support suggested.
Perrotta, P., & Meacham, J.A. (1982).	* N=21 * Mean Age =77 * community resid into 3 grps of 7 * Met 5 sessions @ 45 min per week.		* Rem. not found an effective short-term ther. intervention. * Neither depression nor self-esteem were affected.
Scates,S.K.H., Randolph,D.L, Gutsch, K., & Knight, H.V. (1986).	* N=50 * grp 1: N=17 Rem * grp 2: N=16 CBT * grp 3: N=17 Activities * 6 sessions @ 1 hr x 3 weeks	* LSIA * STAI (State-Trait Anxiety Inventory)	* Remin. may relate:: decr in state anxiety * Results NS, but reminiscence group improved more than others.

Invitation To Participate

APPENDIX B

Dear Ball State University Retiree,

I am a doctoral candidate in counseling psychology requesting your participation in a study on reminiscence and its value and effect on later life adjustment demands. You were identified as a potential research participant in this study by the Ball State *B* Book because of your status as a retired university faculty or staff person. I am interested in hearing you tell the stories from your life. Your participation in this research will be very valuable because it will contribute to our understanding of the resolution of adjustment issues of older adults - how the opportunity to tell one's personal stories and reminiscence in a responsive group of listeners may affect that resolution process. We are eager to investigate the value of such a time honored and naturally occurring theme as "talking about old times" and its potentially therapeutic effect on supporting - or restoring - relief from depression, helplessness, and sense of loss that often seem to afflict many retired persons.

If your choose to participate, your participation will involve, first, returning the enclosed *Informed Consent Form* with your signature and best times and days to contact you for an initial 15 minute telephone interview. At the time of the phone call you will have an opportunity to find out more details of the study. In appreciation of your supportive participation in the study, you will have the opportunity to choose to enter a pool for 1 or 4 $50 cash gifts to be awarded by random selection.

After we talk on the phone, if your are interested in continued involvement in the study, your participation will then involve completing a questionnaire and mailing it back to me in an enclosed self-addressed envelope. The survey takes between 30-45 minutes to complete. Your return of the completed survey will then place you in a second pool for 1 of 4 additional $50 cash gifts. Also, at that time you will become part of a pool of screened volunteer participants from which two reminiscence/ story telling groups will be created. Many retired adults have benefited from groups such as these-finding greater self-awareness, while giving and receiving support from others who are similar to themselves.

Your participation is strictly voluntary. You may choose not to participated or to discontinue participation at any time. Your identity will not be revealed in any report or publication resulting from this research. In order to protect your confidentiality, all your correspondence and responses will be coded by subject number rather than name. Thank you in advance for giving to me of your valuable time.

Sincerely,

Steven Koffman, doctoral candidate,   Donald Nicholas, Ph.D.
Counseling Psychology,   Professor, Counseling Psychology
Principal Investigator   Faculty Supervisor/
                                              Dissertation Chair

<u>Information for Participants and Informed Consent Form</u>

APPENDIX C

The Purpose of this research project entitled "Structured Reminiscence and Gestalt Life Review: Group Treatment of Older Adults for Late Life Adjustment" examines how telling one's own life stories/ narratives in a supportive group may contribute to our understanding of the resolution of adjustment issues (such as depression, loss, helplessness) of older adults. For this project you will be asked first to complete a telephone interview (about 15 minutes) which will provide basic information and allow you to have your questions answered. Following that, you will be asked to complete a series of questionnaires (30-45 minutes) about your current activities, thoughts, and feelings. At that time you will become part of a pool of screened volunteer participants from which two reminiscence/ story telling groups will be created. If you choose to join one of the groups, they will meet for 8 weeks for 1 1/2 hour sessions.

You will not write your name on any of the questionnaires. All data will be coded and remain completely confidential, known only to the investigator. Your name will not be used in any future publication or presentation.

The foreseeable risks from participating in this study are minimal. There is a small possibility that emotional reactions that could result from discussing one's life stories or from reminiscence might have some disturbing quality - such as thoughts or feelings of sadness or anxiety. There are counseling services available to you through the Ball State Practicum Clinic, 285-8047.

There are several benefits to be expected from participation in this study. Your participation in this project will be a valued contribution to our understanding of the resolution of adjustment issues of older adults. Additionally, you will learn about psychological research and gain some insight into your own behavior, feelings and thoughts. In appreciation of your supportive participation in the study, you can choose to enter the first pool for 1 of 4 cash gifts of $50 to be awarded by random selection.

Participation in this study is voluntary and you are free to withdraw your consent and to discontinue participation in this study at any time without prejudice from the investigator.

Please feel free to ask any questions of the investigator before signing this Informed Consent form and beginning the study, as well as at any other time during the study. (work) 285-1736   (home) 214-1010.

For one's rights as a research participant, the following persons may be contacted: Ms. Sandra Smith, Coordinator of Research Compliance, Office of Academic Research and Sponsored Programs, BSU, Muncie, IN 47306, (765) 285-1600. or Dr. Barbara Rothlisberg, Chairperson of the Institutional Review Board, Dept. of Educational Psychology, Ball State University, Muncie, IN 47306, (765) 285-8500.

. . . .
(please sign and return)

I, _____ agree to participate in this study entitled, "Structured Reminiscence and Gestalt Life Review: Group Treatment of Older Adults for Late Life Adjustment." I have had the study clearly explained to me and any questions I have had were answered to my satisfaction. I have read this description of the study and give my consent to participate. I understand that I will receive a copy of this consent form to keep for future reference.

_____   _____
Participant's Signature   Date

_____   _____
Best Times/Days to Contact by Telephone   Telephone #

I choose to enter the pool for 1 of 4 cash gifts of $50 to be awarded.

Yes_____ No _____

Principal Investigator: Faculty Supervisor/ Dissertation Chair:
   Steven Koffman,   Dr. Donald Nicholas
   Counseling Psychology, TC 622   Counseling Psychology, TC 622
   Ball State University   Ball State University
   Muncie, IN 47306   Muncie, IN 47306
   Telephone: (765) 285-8040   Telephone: (765) 285-8040

Dear Ball State University Retiree,

Recently I sent you a letter inviting you to join us in a study on reminiscence and the potential value of telling one's life stories. I thought that having further information may help you to decide if you would like to participate. I want you to know that no assumptions are being made about you or your psychological state, other than that you are probably representative of other retired adults in the community. I hope you will respond affirmatively to this invitation as your unique response is valued and will contribute to the understanding of adjustment issues for older adults.

With your permission, we are looking forward to contacting you for a brief 15 minute telephone interview. Please note - you may always choose to discontinue participation at any time. In appreciation of your support of this study, you will have the choice to enter a pool for 1 of 4 $50 cash gifts.

If you no longer have my original letter regarding this study and are interested, please telephone me at 214-1010 and I will gladly send you another introduction letter, informed consent formand reply envelope.
Sincerely,

Steve Koffman

<u>Cover Letter To Clergy of Delaware County</u>

APPENDIX E

May 26, 1997

Dear

I am working on my doctoral dissertation at Ball State University. The study is on the value of reminiscence for older adults. Enclosed, you will find several copies of an announcement/ advertisement that I have placed in this month's *Prime Years* magazine here in Muncie. I'm asking for <u>your</u> help in contacting additional older persons who, in your judgement, might enjoy and/or benefit from participation in this study.

My intention in contacting you directly is to maximize the chance that all older persons in this community, who would like to participate, have the opportunity. Please read this announcement yourself, and then either post it where it may be seen, read it to your congregation (or associates), or distribute copies as you deem it to be appropriate. If you decide to share this information with your congregation members, please emphasize the need to respond by mid-June.

If you would like to speak to me before making a decision on this, please telephone me at 214-1010 and I will gladly respond to your questions (or possible concerns) about the study.

Thank You,

Steve Koffman

Display Advertisement for Groups

APPENDIX F

An Invitation for Older Adults

....to Reminisce and to Tell Your Stories....

I am doing a dissertation study at Ball State University on reminiscence and the potential value of telling one's life stories. No assumptions are being made about you or your psychological state ....only that you are probably similar to other persons of retirement age in this community. Your unique responses will be valued and will contribute to our understanding of adjustment issues for older adults.

I would like to talk with you for a brief 15 minute telephone interview which will give you the opportunity to find out further details of the study and your potential role. In appreciation of your participation, you will have the option to enter a drawing for 1 of 4 $50 cash prizes. Be assured that your participation will be 100% confidential, and that your name will never be published in connection to this study. Also know that you retain the right to discontinue participation at any time.

If you are interested, please telephone me, Steve Koffman, at 214-1010 or 285-1736. I will send you a consent form and reply envelope and we can then arrange the 15 minute interview at your convenience.

please post or distribute copies of this notice
time limited announcement: expires as of June 15, 1997

Telephone Screen / Interview Protocols (adapted from Crose, 1996)

APPENDIX G

subject name:_____ID code #:____phone:_____

sex: M   F   best days / times to call: _____

address correction:_____

interviewed by:_____ date of interview:_____

*   *   *   *   *begin interview here*   *   *   *

Hello ____name____ , I am _____ . I am calling you at this time for a telephone interview in response to the letter you returned regarding your participation in a doctoral dissertation research project about the value reminiscence for older adults.   Is this a convenient time now to talk or would you prefer to talk at another time? (If OK, proceed; if not OK make another telephone date: * call back on _____ at _____).

How would you like me to call you? _____.   I'd like to begin by saying thank you for your interest and for your response to the letter. By your reply, your name is in a pool for 1 of 4 $50 cash awards. This telephone interview is the first part of your participation and it should take about 15 minutes of your time.

Now I need to get a little information- and I'll ask you some pre-arranged questions. Now some of the questions I'm going to ask may sound a bit silly- but if you will just bear with me. We are trying to get some standard information from people like yourself. If you have some questions for me at any time, you are welcome to ask. OK?   Then, here we go.

Do you mind telling me your age,_____? (Y/N _____)   What is your age? (_____)
Now...., what year would that be that you were you born? (*act confused) (_____)Thank you.

What is the name of your home town? (_____) and when did you come to Muncie?(_____)

_____ , How many years of formal schooling did you have? (_____) HS (____) Coll/Univ (____) Postgrad (_____) and what was your occupation? (_____)

Do you mind telling me a little information about your marital status?
(Y/N_____) S M D W ReM other
Have you had any previous experience with counseling? (Y/N _____)
(*if Yes, then ask if it was:) group?(_____) individual?(_____) something
other?(_____)
So, _____ , what is your favorite season of the year? (_____)
Well, how are you feeling about this season? (_____
_____)

What is your diet like? (_____)
Can you give me an example from one of your meals today? (_____
_____)
How have you been sleeping lately? (_____
_____)

Tell me, , do you ever think about people or things that happened to you in
the past? (Y/ N)
What concerns, if any, do you have about your memory? (*let them tell you/
see how they are thinking about it) _____
_____
_____
_____
_____
_____
_____

Do you mind if we do a little memory test? (Y/N _____)   I am going to give
you 3 things to remember.   (1st is the color, blue ; 2nd is the shape of a
state, California ; 3rd is the concept, honesty.) Blue, California, Honesty.
Will you repeat them back to me? ("_____ ")
(*if needed, repeat this again : "_____")

Do you keep up on current events? (Y/N ____)
What's the most interesting thing in the news today?) _____
_____
_____
_____
_____
_____

After we finish this phone interview, _____ , we will be sending you some questionnaires (like a survey) in the mail. These forms will take about 30 minutes of your time. I'll then ask you to return them to me in the pre-stamped return envelopes which are included for your convenience. Now, your responses to these questionnaires are very important. After you and the rest of the people who responded to the original letter return the written forms, there will be another random selection of people who will be invited to participate in groups. These will be storytelling-reminiscence type groups where people like you will be invited to talk about their own life experiences.

Where we will be doing the groups is at Lucina Hall, right on the Ball State campus here in Muncie. Have you been there lately? (Y/N _____) Do you know where Lucina Hall is located? (Y/N ___)
(*if Yes, act confused and say:)
Can you tell me what roads you would take to get there from your place?
(_____
_____)

(*if No, describe the location of Lucina Hall and say:)
Lucina Hall is on University Ave. That's to the East of Ball Memorial Hospital on University. Across the street from Burris, and to the west from the Student center, between McKinley and Tillotson.
(and then, act confused and say:)
Can you tell me what roads you would take to get there from your place?
(_____
_____)

_____ , we talked a few minutes ago about a memory test and I gave 3 things to remember. Can you tell me what they were?
(Blue Y/N ___ ; California Y/N ___ ; Honesty Y/N ___)

Well, I'm very grateful for your willingness to be a participant in this research. This is a real help for (Steve Koffman) in completing his degree. When you get the questionnaire in the mail in a few days, there will be more of a description of what we are doing- and of your role. Do you have any questions for me at this time? Remember, you will always be free to withdraw from participation at any time. Also, be assured that your privacy will be honored, that your name will not be made public. Let me check your address information once again: Thank you!

additional comments:

IADL IN TELEPHONE SCREENING

APPENDIX G (continued)

(*note to interviewer: insert this IADL section into the Telephone Screen/
Interview Protocols *halfway down the first page - just before "Do you mind
telling me your age?")*

"I have a few questions for you about some activities that we all need to do
as a part of our daily lives. Will you please tell me if you can do these
activities without any help at all, or if you need some help to do them, or if
you can't do them at all."

"Do you have any difficulty using the telephone or making a telephone call?"
(*circle score of 2, 1, or 0 according to their answer)

> 2 without help, including looking up numbers and dialing,

> 1 with some help (can answer phone or dial operator in an emergency,
> but need a special phone or help in getting the number or dialing,

> 0 or are you completely unable to use the phone?

"Do you have any problems getting to places out of walking distance?"

> 2 without help (can travel alone on buses, taxis, or drive own car)

> 1 with some help (need someone to help you or go with you when
> traveling),

> 0 or are you unable to travel unless emergency arrangements are made
> for a specialized vehicle like an ambulance?

if answered by previous question, omit this item. "Can you walk comfortably?"

> 2 without help (except from a cane),

> 1 with some help (either from a person or with the use of a walker, or
> crutches or a walker)

> 0 or are you completely unable to walk?

"How is your vision these days?"

    2 Can you see without help (except for glasses)

    1 with some moderate restrictions or limitations

    0 or is your vision impaired severely or totally?

"Tell me about your hearing..."

    2 Can you hear without help

    1 moderately impaired but can hear with the help of some device (such as a hearing aid)

    0 or is your hearing impaired severely or totally?

"Is there someone who you would ask to help you if you were sick or disabled?" ("for example a husband or wife, a relative, a friend, or a professional care giver?")

    2 Yes, there is someone I would ask who would take care of me as long as needed.

    1 Yes, there is someone I would ask who would help me now and then.

    0 No, there is no one I would ask for help.

                                           "thank you"

Pre-Testing and Screening Package

APPENDIX H

Dear Participant,

Thank you again for your continued interest in this study on the value and impact of reminiscence. As we talked about on the telephone, here is the follow-up set of questionnaires. They should take between 30-45 minutes to fill them out. Please return the surveys as soon as possible. A postage paid reply envelope has been provided for your completed forms-which include the following:

1) The SCL-90 "Symptom Checklist"
2) Sections 1: Life Review Pre-Group Questionnaire (blue page)
3) Sections 2, 3 & 4 (green page)

Remember, all your responses are protected by confidentiality- your name is not connected to the answers of the survey items in any way. Your ID number has been entered on a confidential list. The reminiscence groups, which will *start after Labor Day*, will be made up of volunteer participants such as yourself who will be selected by random procedure. If you are not among those participants who are assigned to the groups, you will be notified and offered an opportunity to participate in a similar group in the near future.

Thank you in advance for your prompt response. Please call 285-1736 (work) or 214-1010 (home) if there are any questions I can answer regarding the study.

Sincerely,

Steve Koffman

SCL-90-R®
Symptom Checklist-90-R

Leonard R. Derogatis, PhD

Last Name	First	MI

ID Number

____   ____   / /
Age   Gender   Test Date

DIRECTIONS:

1. Print your name, · identification number, age, gender, and testing date in the area on the left side of this page.

2. Use a lead pencil only and make a dark mark when responding to the items on pages 2 and 3.

3. If you want to change an answer, erase it carefully and then fill in your new choice.

4. Do not make any marks outside the circles.

**DO NOT SEND TO NATIONAL COMPUTER SYSTEMS
USE ONLY FOR HAND SCORING**

Product Number
05618

Dependent Variables: GDS, LSIA, IBT, EIS

LIsted below are 30 questions which might describe how you have been feeling about various things. Choose the best answer for how you felt over this past week, marking a **circle** around **yes** or **no**. It is not necessary to think over any item very long. Be sure to mark how you actually feel about the statement, not how you think you should feel. There are no right or wrong answers. Please be sure to answer all questions.

Section 1: (GDS)

1. Are you basically satisfied with your life? — yes no
2. Have you dropped many of your activities and interests? — yes no
3. Do you feel that your life is empty? — yes no
4. Do you often get bored? — yes no
5. Are you hopeful about the future? — yes no
6. Are you bothered by thoughts that you can't get out of your head? — yes no
7. Are you in good spirits most of the time? — yes no
8. Are you afraid that something bad is going to happen to you? — yes no
9. Do you feel happy most of the time? — yes no
10. Do you often feel helpless? — yes no
11. Do you often get restless and fidgity? — yes no
12. Do you prefer to stay home, rather than going out doing new things? — yes no
13. Do you frequently worry about the future? — yes no
14. Do you feel you have more problems with your memory than most? — yes no
15. Do you think it is wonderful to be alive now? — yes no
16. Do you often feel downhearted and blue? — yes no
17. Do you feel pretty worthless the way you are now? — yes no
18. Do you worry a lot about the past? — yes no
19. Do you find life very exciting? — yes no
20. Is it hard for you to get started on new projects? — yes no
21. Do you feel full of energy? — yes no
22. Do you feel that your situation is hopeless? — yes no
23. Do you think that most people are better off than you are? — yes no
24. Do you frequently get upset over little things? — yes no
25. Do you frequently feel like crying? — yes no
26. Do you have trouble concentrating? — yes no
27. Do you enjoy getting up in the morning? — yes no
28. Do you prefer to avoid social gatherings? — yes no
29. Is it easy for you to make decisions? — yes no
30. Is your mind as clear as it used to be? — yes no

Here are some statements about life in general that people feel or think differently about. Read each statement and indicate your **agreement** or **disagreement** with these statements. **Circle** the best answer for how you felt over this past week.

Section 2:   (LSIA)

	agree				disagree	
1. I've gotten more breaks in life than most people I know.	1	2	3	4	5	6
2. I am just as happy as when I was younger.	1	2	3	4	5	6
3. My life could be happier than it is now.	1	2	3	4	5	6
4. These are the best years of my life.	1	2	3	4	5	6
5. Most of the things I do are boring or monotonous.	1	2	3	4	5	6
6. I expect some interesting and pleasant things to happen to me in the future.	1	2	3	4	5	6
7. The things I do are as interesting to me as they ever were.	1	2	3	4	5	6
8. I feel old and sometimes tired.	1	2	3	4	5	6
9. I would not change my past life even if I could.	1	2	3	4	5	6
10. I've gotten pretty much what I expected out of life.	1	2	3	4	5	6

Section 3:   (IBT)

	agree				disagree	
1. "A zebra cannot change his stripes."	1	2	3	4	5	6
2. Its almost impossible to overcome influences of the past.	1	2	3	4	5	6
3. The impact of the past does not last forever.	1	2	3	4	5	6
4. People overvalue the influence of the past.	1	2	3	4	5	6
5. If I'd had different experiences, I'd be more like I want to be.	1	2	3	4	5	6
6. I seldom think of past experiences as affecting me now.	1	2	3	4	5	6
7. We are the slaves to our personal histories.	1	2	3	4	5	6
8. Once something strongly affects your life, it always will.	1	2	3	4	5	6
9. People never change basically.	1	2	3	4	5	6
10. I don't look upon the past with any regrets.	1	2	3	4	5	6

Section 4:   (EIS)

	agree				disagree	
1. I am discontented with life.	1	2	3	4	5	6
2. I wish I could change myself.	1	2	3	4	5	6
3. I am proud of what I have done.	1	2	3	4	5	6
4. I would not change my life if I lived it over.	1	2	3	4	5	6
5. I am satisfied with my life so far.	1	2	3	4	5	6
6. Life is too short.	1	2	3	4	5	6
7. I accept myself the way I am.	1	2	3	4	5	6
8. I am willing to take responsibility for my decisions.	1	2	3	4	5	6
9. I regret the mistakes I've made.	1	2	3	4	5	6
10. I worry about getting old.	1	2	3	4	5	6

Facilitators' Manual for Reminiscence Groups

and

Group Protocols: Outline of Technical Content for Structured Reminiscence

Life Review and Gestalt Life Review Groups (Sessions 1- 8)

APPENDIX I

TABLE of CONTENTS

GLR: Session 8   21

Ice Breaker Exercise   22-5

Structured Reminiscence Life Review Groups (SRLR1 and SRLR2)

SRLR Session 1.

Leader tasks and facilitation needs for the initial meeting begin with a welcome statement and session agenda:

1. State group purpose & importance of study, appreciation for participants' willingness and committment to the study. Restate 8 week format, check on parking permits, unique needs of any participants, importance of contacting the group if a session will be "unavoidably missed".

2. Agreement to mutual confidentiality: Need to establish and maintain a trustworthy and safe group environment is a shared responsibility. An example to share might be: "while someone is reminiscing or telling one of their stories, some emotion may be raised-who can say- maybe some sadness or upset feelings might show- let's agree to make that OK." Sign "confidentiality agreement", understanding that sessions are audiotaped.

3. Leaders role model appropriate interpersonal group behavior norms such as avoiding   crosstalk, advice giving, monopolizing group time. Provide group members attentive   listening, support, empathy, respect, patience, validation of common ground.

4. Structured Group Activity:
     1. "People Bingo" as ice breaker: building group cohesion, safety.
     2. Participants pair off (if odd number, process observer might fill role) and "interview" each other.   Followed by mutual introduction of members: (making the rounds).
     3. (again making the rounds) Initiate SRLR process by providing examples of stem/ open ended leads:
          a. "Something about me that you couldn't know unless I told you is...
          b. "Would you begin by telling me your earliest memory?".

5. Explain structure of "homework: (Handout #1)
     1. Find some music (a casette or CD) or art, momento or photograph, that means something to you, provokes a reminiscence, stimulate a memory or story to tell.

2. At home, relax and listen to the music or look at the memory object.
3. Bring it to the next group meeting, if you'd like to share it...or a reminiscence...or a story from your own life.

6. _Sensory Integrative exercise_: (Guided imagery/ progressive relaxation, etc.)

example: "Everyone visualizes: daydreams and memoriesare all types of visualization. You can harness your visualizations and consciously use them to help you with relaxation and in reminiscence. The focus of this exercise is to introduce you to - or to practice - guided visual imagery.

You will be guided through a series of exercises...   Now - Gently and comfortably close your eyes. I would like you to imagine yourself in a dimly lit room, seated in a very comfortable chair. Allow yourself to relax yourself into the most comfortable position in the chair   - perhaps there is some relaxing music in the background or maybe it is just quiet. It is a place that you feel very secure... and now...let yourself inhale your breath deeply...and then exhale completely .   Again, take a deep breath--easy in and easy out. and one more time inhale deeply...easy in and then exhale easy out.

Concentrate on the muscles of your toes and feet. Relax them all the way- making them limp and heavy, and getting slightly warmer as they relax. Experience the tension flowing out of those muscles as you let go more and more...and the more you let go the better you'll feel. and one more time inhale deeply...easy in and then exhale easy out. *(pause x5 sec)*

Now concentrate on your leg and thigh muscles...make them limp and heavy and warm..   Observe the tension flowing out of those muscles as they relax more and more and experience that feeling of calm and well being. and one more time inhale deeply...easy in and then exhale easy out. *(pause x5 sec)*

Turn now to the muscles in your stomach, your chest, and your back. Focus on making those muscles limp and heavy and warm. Note the tension flowing out completely leaving you with a feeling of pure relaxation. and one more time inhale deeply... then exhale easy out. *(pause x5 sec)*

Now move to your shoulders and down your arms to your hands and fingers. Relax those muscles all the way and experience the tension flowing out of them. Feel them getting heavier and warmer as you concentrate on relaxing more and more.   And inhale deeply... then exhale easy out. *(pause x5 sec)*

Next, move to the head and neck, and relax all those muscles. Pay particular attention to the muscles in the back of your neck, the muscles around your eyes, the jaw muscles, the forehead, and the temples. Just let go more and more and note the tension flowing out of all the neck and head muscles. Note the sensation of calm and hold that memory as you relax more and more .... and one more time inhale deeply.....easy in and then exhale easy out. *(pause x5 sec)*

Now, pay attention to your relaxed body, and your open relaxed breathing. As your mind is relaxed and your thoughts are clear- Memories can come to you clearly when you relax like this. Remember this feeling - know that you can come back another time to this safe and secure place.

Now again, relax your body and breathe deeply. As I count from 10 to 1 stay relaxed and breathing deeply....

10...9 - as I count down, return to the here and now of this room.
8...7 - as the count down gets to 1 you can open your eyes,
6...5 - remember about your body's reaction to guided visualization
4...3 - return your awareness to this room and the reminiscence group
2...1 - as you open your eyes, feel refreshed and alert."

7. Make the rounds again as group closure.

Reminiscence Group: Handout #1

1. Find some music (a casette or CD) or art, momento or photograph, that means something to you, provokes a reminiscence, stimulate a memory or a story to tell. At home, relax and listen to the music or look at the memory object.

2. Bring it to the next group meeting, if you'd like to share it...or a reminiscence...or a story from your own life.

Reminiscence Prompts:
1. Would you begin by telling me your earliest memory?
2. Were you ever sick as a child?   Who took care of you?
3. What are some of your favorite memories as a child?
4. Was there a special person or group that strongly influenced your early life? Who was that person? What can you tell me about them?
5. Describe your family, parents and siblings, as you saw them as a child?
6. What did you like about being a girl or a boy?
7. Can you tell me the meaning of your family name?
8. How did your parents meet?
9. What was the first house you remember like? The street you lived on.
10. What were your favorite foods as a child? Where did the recipes come from?
11. Tell me about the pets you had as a child.
12. What were your favorite pastimes as a teenager?
13. What was an important change that happened to you as a teenager?
14. What do you remember about your first boyfriend/ girlfriend?
15. Tell me about your first job.   Did you like it?
16. What was the happiest birthday you can recall?
17. What was the most memorable present you ever received?
18. What part did religion play in your growing up?
19. Tell me about an experience of "love at first sight".
20. What first attracted you to the person you married?
21. What surprised you about being married?
22. What kinds of things did you and your spouse face together?
23. How would you sum up your life in one or two words?
     Why did you choose those words?
24. What would you like the chance to do over?

25. What would you change about your life?
26. What was the most interesting period of history that you lived through?
27. What was your greatest disappointment or achievement?
28. Could you tell me about the most difficult thing you had to deal with in your life? What about your moment of greatest joy?
29. Did you ever make changes in your life? Divorce?   Switch careers? Move a great distance? Why did you decide to make this change?
30. What advice did your parents give you? Did you hand down the same advice to your children? Why? Why not?
31. What is the biggest difference between your childhood and that of your children? Your grandchildren?
32. Have you ever received a special honor or medal?

SRLR Session 2.

All meetings will begin with leaders welcome, sensory intergative exercise relaxation and repeat of some stem prompts from Handout #1, then a series of "making the rounds". Leaders' role is maintenance of safe environment for disclosure, empathic, supportive listening. Members will engage in reporting of homework experience, followed by introductory structured life review exercise. All groups close with final check-in.

Homework (see Handout #2):

Reminiscence Group: Handout #2

1. Using some of the same techniques as last week (or in your own style), find a memory or recall a story from your childhood years: such as family, school, church, culture, parents, siblings, friends, events, sports, travel.

2. At home, relax and listen to the music or look at the memory object.

3. Bring it to the next group meeting, if you'd like to share it...or a reminiscence...or a story from your own life.

Childhood Reminiscence Prompts:

1. What is the very first thing you can remember in your life? Go as far back as you can.
2. What other things can you remember about when you were very young?
3. What was life like for you as a child?
4. What were your parents like? What were their weaknesses, strengths?
5. Did you have any brothers or sisters? Tell me what each was like.
6. Did someone close to you die when you were growing up?

7. Did someone important to you go away?
8. Do you remember ever being very sick?
9. Do you remember having an accident?
10. Do you remember being in a very dangerous situation?
11. Was there anything that was important to you that was lost or destroyed?

SRLR Session 3.

All meetings will begin with leaders welcome, sensory intergative exercise relaxation and repeat of some stem prompts from Handout #2: **Childhood**, then a series of "making the rounds". Leaders' role is maintenance of safe environment for disclosure, empathic, supportive listening. Members will engage in reporting of homework experience, followed by introductory structured life review exercise. All groups close with final check-in.

Homework (see Handout #3):

Reminiscence Group: Handout #3

1. Using some of the same techniques as last week (or in your own style), find a memory or recall a story from your adolescence.

2. At home, relax and listen to the music or look at the memory object.

3. Bring it to the next group meeting, if you'd like to share it...or a reminiscence...or a story from your own life.

Adolescence Reminiscence Prompts:
1. When you think about yourself and your life as a teenager, what is the first thing your can remember about that time?
2. What other things stand out in your memory about being a teenager?
3. Who were the important people for you? Tell me about them Parents, brothers and sisters, friends, teachers, those you were especially close to, those you admired, those you wanted to be like.
4. Did you go to school? What did school mean for you at that time?
5. Did you work during these years?
6. Tell me of any hardships you experienced at this time.
7. Do you remember feeling that there wasn't enough food or necessities of life as a child or adolescent?
8. Do you remember feeling left alone, abandoned, not having enough love or care as a child or adolescent?
9. What were the pleasant things about your adolescence?
10. What was the most unpleasant thing about your adolescence?
11. All things considered, would you say your were happy or unhappy as a teenager?

SRLR Session 4.

All meetings will begin with leaders welcome, sensory intergative exercise relaxation and repeat of some stem prompts from Handout #3: *Adolescence*, then a series of "making the rounds". Leaders' role is maintenance of safe environment for disclosure, empathic, supportive listening. Members will engage in reporting of homework experience, followed by introductory structured life review exercise. All groups close with final check-in.

Homework (see Handout #4):

Reminiscence Group: Handout #4

1. Using some of the same techniques as last week (or in your own style), find a memory or recall a story from your family and home.

2. At home, relax and listen to the music or look at the memory object.

3. Bring it to the next group meeting, if you'd like to share it...or a reminiscence...or a story from your own life.

Family and Home Reminiscence Prompts:

1. How did your parents get along?
2. How did other people in you home get along?
3. What was the atmosphere in your home?
4. Were you punished as a child? For what? Who did the punishing? Who was the "boss"?
5. When you wanted something from your parents, how did you go about getting it?
6. What kind of person did your parents like the most? The least?
7. Who were you closest to in your family?
8. Who in your family were you most like? In what way?

SRLR Session 5.

All meetings will begin with leaders welcome, sensory intergative exercise relaxation and repeat of some stem prompts from Handout #4: *Family and Home*, then a series of "making the rounds". Leaders' role is maintenance of safe environment for disclosure, empathic, supportive listening. Members will engage in reporting of homework experience, followed by introductory structured life review exercise. All groups close with final check-in.

Homework (see Handout #5):

Reminiscence Group: Handout #5

1. Using some of the same techniques as last week (or in your own style), find a memory or recall a story from your adulthood

2. At home, relax and listen to the music or look at the memory object.

3. Bring it to the next group meeting, if you'd like to share it...or a reminiscence...or a story from your own life.

Adulthood Reminiscence Prompts:
1. Now I'd like you to think about your life as an adult starting when you were in your twenties up to today. Tell me of the most important events that happened to you in your adulthood.
2. What was life like for you in your twenties and thirties?
3. What kind of person were you? What did you enjoy?
4. Tell me about your work. Did you enjoy your work? Did you earn and adequate living? Did you work hard during those years? Were you appreciated?
5. Did you marry? (if yes) What kind of person is or was your spouse? (if no) Why not?
6. Do you think marriages get better or worse over time?
7. Were you married more than once?
8. On the whole, would you say you had a happy or unhappy marriage?
9. What were some of main difficulties you encountered during your adult years?
   a.   Did someone close to you die? Go away?
   b.   Were you ever sick? Have an accident?
   c.   Did you move often? Change jobs?
   d.   Did you ever feel alone? Abandoned?
   e.   Did you ever feel need?

SRLR Session 6.

All meetings will begin with leaders welcome, sensory intergative exercise relaxation and repeat of some stem prompts from Handout #5: *Adulthood*, then a series of "making the rounds". Leaders' role is maintenance of safe environment for disclosure, empathic, supportive listening. Members will engage in reporting of homework experience, followed by introductory structured life review exercise. All groups close with final check-in.

Homework (see Handout #6):

Reminiscence Group: Handout #6

1. Using some of the same techniques as last week (or in your own style), find a memory or recall a story from your work, career, or relationships.

2. At home, relax and listen to the music or look at the memory object.

3. Bring it to the next group meeting, if you'd like to share it...or a reminiscence...or a story from your own life.

Work, Career,or Relationships Reminiscence Prompts:

1. In your career, you must have exerted a lot of effort.
2. Help me understand what it was like for you when you worked as a_____.
3. What gave you the greatest satisfaction while you were working at _____?
4. What was the most difficult part of your work/ aspect of your career at _____?
5. When did you get married?
6. Were there other big moments in your married life or single life?
7. How would your children describe you as a mother or a father? a grandmother? or a grandfather? as an aunt or an uncle?

SRLR Session 7.

All meetings will begin with leaders welcome, sensory intergative exercise relaxation and repeat of some stem prompts from Handout #6: *Work, Career, Relationships*, then a series of "making the rounds". Leaders' role is maintenance of safe environment for disclosure, empathic, supportive listening. Members will engage in reporting of homework experience, followed by structured life review exercise.

Homework   (see Handout #7): **Reminiscence Group: Handout #7**

We have one last meeting next week. We've been talking about your life for quite some time now. For homework, consider your over-all feelings and ideas about your life with some of the following ideas as Summary Reminiscence prompts:

1. What are some of the milestones that stand out in your life as you look back?
2. What one thing (object, person, idea, event, achievement) do you prize the most at this time in your life?
3. What do you like most about yourself?
4. What do you see as your most significant contribution to your family?
5. What do you see as your most significant contribution to the next generation?
6. Did you form significant relationships with other people?
7. On the whole what kind of life do you think you've had?
8. If everything were to be the same would you like to live your live over again?
9. If you were going to live your life over again, what would you change? Leave unchanged?
10. What would you say the main satisfactions in you life have been? (Try for three). (Why were they satisfying)?
11. Everyone has had disappointments. What were the main disappointments in your life?
12. What was the hardest thing you had to face in your life? Describe.
13. What was the happiest period of your life?   What about it made it the happiest period? Why is your life less happy now?
14. What was the unhappiest period of your life? Why is your life happier now?
15. What was the proudest moment in your life?
16. If you could stay the same age all your life, what age would you choose? Why?
17. How do you think you've made out in life? Better or worse than what you hoped for?
18. Let's talk a little about you as you are now. What are the best things about the age you are now?
19. What are the worst things about being the age you are now?
20. What are the most important things to you in your life today?
21. What do you hope will happen to you as you grow older?
22. What do you fear will happen to you as you grow older?
23. Have you enjoyed participating in this review of your life?

SRLR Session 8.

Summary and Integration of Life Review/ Reminiscence. Termination of the group, post-testing distributed, collected. Theme this meeting: **Summary and Termination** (refer to Handout #7)

We've been talking about you life for quite some time now. Let's discuss your over-all feelings and ideas about your life.

Closure and post-testing distributed, collected.

Gestalt Life Review Groups (GLR1 and GLR2)

GLR Session 1.

Leader tasks and facilitation needs for the initial meeting begin with a welcome statement and session agenda:

1. State group purpose & importance of study, appreciation for participants' willingness and committment to the study. Statement of group as opportunity to talk through or resolve some old issues

2. Agreement to mutual confidentiality: The stories that others tell and expressions of feelings must remain within the group. Need to establish and maintain a trustworthy and safe group environment is a shared responsibility.

3. Leaders role model appropriate interpersonal group behavior norms such as avoiding crosstalk, advice giving, monopolizing group time.

4. Provide group members support, empathy, respect, while facilitating sensory integrative, awareness, grounding experience in movement to here and now engagement, intensifying affect awareness in present.
    Summary: therapist actively directs/facilitates group psychotherapeutic intervention (vs SRLR "client centered model")

5. Structured Group Activity:
    1. "People Bingo" as ice breaker: building group cohesion, safety.
    2. Participants pair off (if odd number, process observer might fill role) and "interview" each other. Followed by mutual introduction of members: (making the rounds).

6. Explain structure of "homework: (Handout #1a)
    1. Find some music (a casette or CD) or art, momento or photograph, that means something to you, provokes a reminiscence, stimulate a memory or story to tell.
    2. At home, relax and listen to the music or look at the memory object.
    3. Bring it to the next group meeting, if you'd like to share it...or a reminiscence...or a story from your own life.
    4. **Become increasingly aware of what you feel "in the here and now" about your memory.**

7. Sensory Integrative exercise: Modeled after Awareness (Stevens, 1971) ex: "The Mirror"- Imagine that you are in a very dark room. You can't see anything yet, but there is a large mirror in front of you. As the room gradually becomes lighter, you will be able to see an image of yourself reflected in the

mirror. The image may be quite different from the image that you usually see, or it might not be. Just look into the darkness and let this image emerge as the light grows brighter...Eventually you will be able to see it quite clearly...What is this image like? What do you notice most about this image?...What is its posture like?...How does it move?...What is its facial expression like?...What feeling or attitude does this image express?...How do you feel about this image?... Now talk silently to this image, and imagine that the image can speak to you...What do you say to the image and what does the image answer?...How do you feel as you speak to this image?

Now trade places, and become the image in the mirror. As this image, what do you say to yourself as you continue the dialogue between you?...Comment on the relationship between you two...See if you can discover even more about your experience of being this image...Continue this conversation between the image and yourself for awhile, and see what else you can discover from each other. Switch back and forth between the two whenever you like, but continue the dialogue and interaction between you...

Now become yourself again, and look again at the image in the mirror...How do you feel now toward this image?...Are there any changes now, compared with when you first saw this image?...Is there anything you want to say to this image beforeyou say goodbye?...Now slowly say goodbye to this image,...and return to your existence in this room, Just stay quietly with your experience for awhile...

8. (Making the rounds) Initiate **GLR** process by providing examples of stem/ open ended leads:
    1. **What are you most aware of now?**
        Continue GLR by providing stem/ open ended leads.
        Examples:
        "Right now, I am most aware of....(feeling, memory, etc.)
        "Would you begin by telling me your earliest memory?"
9. Make the rounds again as group closure.

**** Outline/ Summary of GLR Group Facilitation Differential:

GLR: Session 1.
    Same theme, stem prompts, (homework form "a") as SRLR Session 1.
    Group facilitation differential:
    1. Provide group members support, empathy, respect,
    2. Movement is directed toward closure of unresolved conflicts, resolution of unfinished business, empowerment of personal responsibility in accord with Gestalt theory and techniques.
        * Integrative, awareness, and focusing techniques of Gestalt.
        * Empty chair, psychodrama, dreamwork techniques.
        * Summary: therapist actively directs/facilitates experiential group psychotherapy intervention (vs SRLR "client centered model")
    3. Sensory Integrative exercise: modeled after Awareness (Stevens,1971)

Reminiscence Group: Handout #1a

1. Find some music, art, momento or photograph that means something to you, provokes a reminiscence, stimulate a memory or a story you might want to tell. At home, relax and listen to the music or look at the memory object.
   2. Bring it to the next group meeting, if you'd like to share it...or a reminiscence...or a story from your own life. Ask yourself: What are you most aware of in that moment...inside yourself (like feelings) or in the outer environment?   Become aware of what you are feeling about your memory.

1. Would you begin by telling me your earliest memory?
2. Were you ever sick as a child?   Who took care of you?
3. What are some of your favorite memories as a child?
4. Was there a special person or group that strongly influenced your early life? Who was that person? What can you tell me about them?
5. Describe your family, parents and siblings, as you saw them as a child?
6. What did you like about being a girl or a boy? Tell about the pets you had.
7. Can you tell me the meaning of your family name?
8. How did your parents meet?
9. What was the first house you remember like? The street you lived on.
10. What were your favorite foods as a child? Where did the recipes come from?
11. What were your favorite pastimes as a teenager?
12. What was an important change that happened to you as a teenager?
13. What do you remember about your first boyfriend/ girlfriend?
14. Tell me about your first job.   Did you like it?
15. What was the happiest birthday you can recall?
16. What was the most memorable present you ever received?
17. What part did religion play in your growing up?
18. Tell me about an experience of "love at first sight".
19. What first attracted you to the person you married?
20. What surprised you about being married?
21. What kinds of things did you and your spouse face together?
22. How would you sum up your life in one or two words?   Why those words?
23. What would you like the chance to do over?
24. What would you change about your life?
25. What was the most interesting period of history that you lived through?
26. What was your greatest disappointment or achievement?
27. Could you tell me about the most difficult thing you had to deal with in your life?   What about your moment of greatest joy?
28. Did you ever make changes in your life? Divorce?   Switch careers? Move a great distance? Why did you decide to make this change?
29. What advice did your parents give you? Did you hand down the same advice to your children?   Why? Why not?
30. What is the biggest difference between your childhood and that of your children? Your grandchildren?

GLR Session 2.

same theme, stem prompts, homework as SRLR Session 2.
Differential Gestalt facilitation of affect and awareness in here and now as emergent in participants' life review process. Techniques used include (but are not limited to)
1. Integrative, awareness, and focusing techniques of Gestalt.
2. Empty chair, psychodrama, dreamwork techniques.
3. Movement is directed toward closure of unresolved conflicts, resolution of unfinished business, empowerment of personal responsibility in accord with Gestalt theory.
  ***Summary: therapist actively directs/facilitates group psychotherapeutic intervention (vs SRLR "client centered model")

Reminiscence Group: Handout #2a

1. Using some of the same techniques as last week (such as listening to some music, looking at photographs or at some momento) - or in your own style- find a memory or recall a story from your **childhood years**: such as family, school, church, culture, parents, siblings, friends, events, sports, travel.

2. At home, as you relax and listen to the music or look at the memory object, become increasingly aware of what you feel "in the here and now" about your memory. Ask yourself a queation like: "What am I most aware of in this moment...inside myself (such as emotions, sensations or impressions) or in the outer environment (like smells or sounds)?" Pay attention to memories, images or feelings that may arise.

Take a look as these examples of **Childhood** reminiscence prompts and questions:
1. What is the very first thing you can remember in your life?
   Go as far back as you can.
2. What other things can you remember about when you were very young?
3. What was life like for you as a child?
4. What were your parents like? What were their weaknesses, strengths?
5. Did you have any brothers or sisters? Tell me what each was like.
6. Did someone close to you die when you were growing up?
7. Did someone important to you go away?
8. Do you remember ever being very sick?
9. Do you remember having an accident?
10. Do you remember being in a very dangerous situation?
11. Was there anything that was important to you that was lost or destroyed?

GLR: Session 3.

Ongoing therapist directed gestaltic processing of life review in group
Same theme, stem prompts, (homework form "a") as SRLR Session 3.

Reminiscence Group: Handout #3a

1. Using some of the same techniques as last week (such as listening to some music, looking at photographs or at some momento) - or in your own style- find a memory or recall a story from your **adolescence years**: such as family, school, church, culture, parents, siblings, friends, events, sports, travel.

2. At home, as you relax and listen to the music or look at the memory object, become increasingly aware of what you feel "in the here and now" about your memory. Ask yourself a queation like: "What am I most aware of in this moment...inside myself (such as emotions, sensations or impressions) or in the outer environment (like smells or sounds)?" Pay attention to memories, images or feelings that may arise.

Take a look as these examples of **Adolescence** reminiscence prompts and questions:

1. When you think about yourself and your life as a teenager, what is the first thing your can remember about that time?
2. What other things stand out in your memory about being a teenager?
3. Who were the important people for you? Tell me about them Parents, brothers and sisters, friends, teachers, those you were especially close to, those you admired, those you wanted to be like.
4. Did you go to school? What did school mean for you at that time?
5. Did you work during these years?
6. Tell me of any hardships you experienced at this time.
7. Do you remember feeling that there wasn't enough food or necessities of life as a child or adolescent?
8. Do you remember feeling left alone, abandoned, not having enough love or care as a child or adolescent?
9. What were the pleasant things about your adolescence?
10. What was the most unpleasant thing about your adolescence?
11. All things considered, would you say your were happy or unhappy as a teenager?

GLR: Session 4.
Ongoing therapist directed gestaltic processing of life review in group
Same theme, stem prompts, (homework form "a") as SRLR Session 4.

Reminiscence Group: Handout #4a

1. Using some of the same techniques as last week (such as listening
to some music, looking at photographs or at some momento) - or in your own
style- find a memory or recall a story from your **family and home**: such as
family, school, church, culture, parents, siblings, friends, events, sports,
travel.

2. At home, as you relax and listen to the music or look at the memory
object, become increasingly aware of what you feel "in the here and now"
about your memory. Ask yourself a queation like: "What am I most aware of
in this moment...inside myself (such as emotions, sensations or impressions)
or in the outer environment (like smells or sounds)?" Pay attention to
memories, images or feelings that may arise.

Take a look as these examples of **Family and Home** reminiscence
prompts and questions:

1. How did your parents get along?
2. How did other people in you home get along?
3. What was the atmosphere in your home?
4. Were you punished as a child? For what? Who did the punishing?
   Who was the "boss"?
5. When you wanted something from your parents, how did you go about
   getting it?
6. What kind of person did your parents like the most? The least?
7. Who were you closest to in your family?
8. Who in your family were you most like? In what way?

GLR: Session 5
Ongoing therapist directed gestaltic processing of life review in group
Same theme, stem prompts, (homework form "a") as SRLR Session 5.

Reminiscence Group: Handout #5a

1. Using some of the same techniques as last week (such as listening
to some music, looking at photographs or at some momento) - or in your own
style- find a memory or recall a story from your **Adulthood**: such as family,
school, church, culture, parents, siblings, friends, events, sports, travel.

2. At home, as you relax and listen to the music or look at the memory
object, become increasingly aware of what you feel "in the here and now"
about your memory. Ask yourself a queation like: "What am I most aware of
in this moment...inside myself (such as emotions, sensations or impressions)
or in the outer environment (like smells or sounds)?" Pay attention to
memories, images or feelings that may arise.

Take a look as these examples of **Adulthood** reminiscence prompts and
questions:
1. Now I'd like you to think about your life as an adult starting when you were in
   your twenties up to today. Tell me of the most important events that
   happened to you in your adulthood.
2. What was life like for you in your twenties and thirties?
3. What kind of person were you? What did you enjoy?
4. Tell me about your work. Did you enjoy your work? Did you earn and
   adequate living? Did you work hard during those years? Were you
      appreciated?
5. Did you marry? (if yes) What kind of person is or was your spouse?
   (if no) Why not?
6. Do you think marriages get better or worse over time?
7. Were you married more than once?
8. On the whole, would you say you had a happy or unhappy marriage?
9. What were some of main difficulties you encountered during your adult
   years?
   a.   Did someone close to you die? Go away?
   b.   Were you ever sick? Have an accident?
   c.   Did you move often? Change jobs?
   d.   Did you ever feel alone? Abandoned?
   e.   Did you ever feel need?

GLR: Session 6
Ongoing therapist directed gestaltic processing of life review in group
Same theme, stem prompts, (homework form "a") as SRLR Session 6.

Reminiscence Group: Handout #6a

1. Using some of the same techniques as last week (such as listening to some music, looking at photographs or at some momento) - or in your own style- find a memory or recall a story from your **work, career, or relationships.**

2. At home, as you relax and listen to the music or look at the memory object, become increasingly aware of what you feel "in the here and now" about your memory. Ask yourself a queation like: "What am I most aware of in this moment...inside myself (such as emotions, sensations or impressions) or in the outer environment (like smells or sounds)?" Pay attention to memories, images or feelings that may arise.

3. Bring it to the next group meeting, if you'd like to share it...or a reminiscence...or a story from your own life.

Take a look as these examples of **Work, Career, or Relationship** reminiscence prompts and questions:

1. In your career, you must have exerted a lot of effort.
2. Help me understand what it was like for you when you worked as a_____.
3. What gave you the greatest satisfaction while you were working at _____ __?
4. What was the most difficult part of your work/ aspect of your career at _____?
5. When did you get married?
6. Were there other big moments in your married life or single life?
7. How would your children describe you as a mother or a father? a grandmother or a grandfather? as an aunt or an uncle?

GLR: Session 7

Ongoing therapist directed gestaltic processing of life review in group
Same theme, stem prompts, (homework form "a") as SRLR Session 7.

Reminiscence Group: Handout #7a

We've been reminiscing and talking about your life for quite some
time now. We have one last meeting next week. Is there something
important to you as a summary story that you wish to share with the group?
For homework this week, consider your over-all feelings and ideas about
your life. Using the same techniques as last week (or in your own style),
consider some of the following ideas of **Summary** reminiscence prompts:

1. What are some of the milestones that stand out in your life as you look back?
2. What one thing (object, person, idea, event, achievement) do you prize the most at this time in your life?
3. What do you like most about yourself?
4. What do you see as your most significant contribution to your family?
5. What do you see as your most significant contribution to the next generation?
6. Did you form significant relationships with other people?
7. On the whole what kind of life do you think you've had?
8. If everything were to be the same would you like to live your live over again?
9. If you were going to live your life over again, what would you change? Leave unchanged?
10. What would you say the main satisfactions in you life have been? (Try for three). (Why were they satisfying)?
11. Everyone has had disappointments. What were your main disappointments?
12. What was the hardest thing you had to face in your life? Describe.
13. What was the happiest period of your life?   What about it made it the happiest period? Why is your life less happy now?
14. What was the unhappiest period of your life? Why is your life happier now?
15. What was the proudest moment in your life?
16. If you could stay the same age all your life, what age would you choose? Why?
17. How do you think you've made out in life? Better or worse than what you hoped for?
18. Let's talk a little about you as you are now. What are the best things about the age you are now?
19. What are the worst things about being the age you are now?
20. What are the most important things to you in your life today?
21. What do you hope will happen to you as you grow older?
22. What do you fear will happen to you as you grow older?
23. Have you enjoyed participating in this review of your life?

GLR: Session 8

Ongoing therapist directed gestaltic processing of life review in group
Same theme, stem prompts, (homework form "a") as SRLR Session 8.
Termination, post-testing procedures as SRLR Session 8.

PEOPLE "BINGO"
Getting To Know Each Other

This is like a person-to-person scavenger hunt - or a game of bingo. Walk around and try to find someone in this group who fits each of these categories. Have them sign their in the box that describes them. Try to get to know everyone here.

B	I	N	G	O
the same color of eyes as you	has sang, danced or performed in front of other people	has lived outside the state of Indiana	has ever played on an athletic team	has seen a U.S. president in person
likes to tell jokes	listened to FDR on the radio	remembers a favorite teacher from their student days	has the same favorite desert as you	has been to the Indy 500
was born in the same month as you	does volunteer work in the community	FREE SPACE	speaks another language fluently	remembers the day they retired
likes the same kind of music as you	remembers their first love	loves old movies	has freckles or has been married to someone with freckles	loves chocolate
has ever enjoyed camping out	likes eating at Chinese restaurants	was the youngest child in their family of origin	can remember their first car	has been to the top of a skyscraper

form A

PEOPLE "BINGO"
Getting To Know Each Other

This is like a person-to-person scavenger hunt - or a game of bingo. Walk around and try to find someone in this group who fits each of these categories. Have them sign their in the box that describes them. Try to get to know everyone here.

B	I	N	G	O
is the parent to two or more children	likes their shoulders massaged	likes eating at Chinese restaurants	has told another person "I love you" in the past week	has ever climbed a mountain
is a cat lover	recalls the day they got their first bicycle	has ever lived with someone from another country	loves to garden	has lived outside the state of Indiana
is a regular walker	has been married more than forty years	FREE SPACE	has seen a movie star in person	likes to tell stories from their past
remembers where they were when Kennedy was shot	has been hugged today	doesn't like birthdays	has ever enjoyed camping out	the same color of eyes as you
has freckles or has been married to someone with freckles	has had a dog for a pet	has ever worked in a restaurant	remembers their first love	likes to drink coffee

form B

PEOPLE "BINGO"
Getting To Know Each Other

This is like a person-to-person scavenger hunt - or a game of bingo. Walk around and try to find someone in this group who fits each of these categories. Have them sign their in the box that describes them. Try to get to know everyone here.

B	I	N	G	O
has had a dog for a pet	likes to drink coffee	can cross their eyes	has ever gone swimming in the ocean	remembers their wedding day
was born in the same month as you	has a relative over 90 years old	lives alone	has been married more than forty years	has been a die hard sports fan
has four or more grandchildren	has taught a class in the past year	**FREE SPACE**	likes the same kind of music as you	is the youngest child in their family of origin
has ever lived in an ethnically or racially diverse community	loves chocolate	has been to the top of a skyscraper	likes to tell jokes	recalls the day they got their first bicycle
has been hugged today	has successfully stopped smoking	loves to garden	has been to the Grand Canyon	has great-grandchildren

form C

PEOPLE "BINGO"
Getting To Know Each Other

This is like a person-to-person scavenger hunt - or a game of bingo. Walk around and try to find someone in this group who fits each of these categories. Have them sign their in the box that describes them. Try to get to know everyone here.

B	I	N	G	O
has the same favorite desert as you	has a longstanding disagreement or problem with a relative	is a cat lover	loves old movies	has successfully stopped smoking
vacation destination would be the same as your own	remembers their first job	was an only child	has great-grandchildren	has read a novel for pleasure within the past two months
can remember their first car	has ever visited another country	**FREE SPACE**	remembers where they were when Kennedy was shot	has a part-time job
has been to the Grand Canyon	remembers the day they retired	four or more grandchildren	can cross their eyes	doesn't like birthdays
has ever worked in a restaurant	likes to tell stories from their past	has sang, danced or performed in front of other people	has a relative over 90 years old	has seen a U.S. president in person

form D

Information for Pilot Group Participants and Informed Consent Form

APPENDIX J

The Purpose of this research project entitled "Structured Reminiscence and Gestalt Life Review: Group Treatment of Older Adults for Late Life Adjustment" examines how telling one's own life stories/ narratives in a supportive group may contribute to our understanding of the resolution of adjustment issues (such as depression, loss, helplessness) of older adults. The purpose of the pilot group exercise is to demonstrate (and to videotape) the structured reminiscence models which are the subject of the study. Your role in this 2 hour (approx) period is that of a retired older adult (age 65 or up). You are free to play yourself- or anyone at all that you would like to role play. You might choose to reminisce about something that actually happened to you- or create a memory from your imagination.

The videotapes of the pilot groups will be viewed by an expert in geropsychology (Mark Minear) for the purpose of conceptual and technical consultation. The transcription will be coded and remain completely confidential, known only to the investigator. Your name will not be used in any future publication or presentation.

The foreseeable risks from participating in the pilot groups are minimal. There is a small possibility that emotional reactions that could result from discussing one's life stories or from reminiscence might have some disturbing quality - such as thoughts or feelings of sadness or anxiety. There are counseling services available to you through the Ball State Practicum Clinic, 285-8047. Your participation in this project will be a contribution to our understanding of the resolution of adjustment issues of older adults. Additionally, you will learn about psychological research and may gain some insight into your own behavior, feelings and thoughts.

I, _____ volunteer to participate in the pilot groups for the study entitled, "Structured Reminiscence and Gestalt Life Review: Group Treatment of Older Adults for Late Life Adjustment." I have had the study clearly explained to me and any questions I have had were answered to my satisfaction. I have read this description of the study and give my consent to participate.

_____
Participant's Signature   Date

_____
Principal Investigator: Steven D. Koffman

Mark Minear: Feedback On Pilot Group Videotapes

APPENDIX K _

September 5, 1997

Regarding: Steve Koffman's dissertation
Reviewer: Mark Minear, Ph.D.

1) After reviewing the video tapes, I would offer the following comments:

In regard to the basic question presented to me according to the protocol of Steve's dissertation, the stated purpose, style, and direction of the two approaches to life review (Structured Reminiscence Life Review [SRLR] and Gestalt Life Review [GLR]) as seen in the video tapes of 7/97 are good and accurate protrayals. The leaders/facilitators would appear to be on the right track according to the designated tasks and goals of the groups and their corresponding therapeutic approaches.

2) The following thoughts highlight what was presented well on the videos. These affirmations are intermingled with suggestions (to push the groups a little more in the direction of the designated approaches) which may or may not be helpful:

The distinctiveness between the two approaches could be understood both in terms of process as well as content. In order to present a contrast between SRLR and GLR, it may be helpful to understand SRLR in terms of a person-centered experience. Those designated as leaders actually function more like "facilitators" who operate in a nondirective fashion. They would maintain the basic reflective responses as the group paves its own way in response to the targeted theme of each session. Paraphrasing, clarifying, and summarizing are techniques which keep the emphasis upon the reminiscence of the group members. Consequently, the tendency will be to focus on pleasant, positive memories and personal strengths in celebration of one's past and history. Such directions are quite acceptable. Facilitators will need to be careful of "probing" and use of techniques which can guide and/or control.

GLR, on the other hand, would more likely have "leaders" (instead of facilitators) who operate in a directive fashion and even "call" upon members at times. They are more likely to probe with the goal of intensifying the experience (immediate awareness of current feelings) in the here and now in order to intergrate the physical behaviors (including bodily sensations), emotions, and cognitions of the group members. Though careful not to be aggressive, it would be accurate to consider the leaders to be assertive as they pursue the unfinished business from the personal histories of the group members. The tendency is to look for "pathology" and focus on brokeness in order to move toward wholeness. There may be an emphasis to focus more on emotions and behaviors and less on cognitions as the leaders challenge group members to take care of old business by taking responsibility of any disowned parts. Action-oriented techniques could include the "hot seat" (perhaps the most famous Gestalt group technique), empty chair (to converse with self or other individuals--living or dead--from the past), fantasy or role play (such as becoming some object or person), overexaggeration of a behavior, staying with the feelings, dream work, and having parts of one's body "speak" for the group member. Exercises are designed to enable participants to become increasingly aware of bodily tensions and of the fear of getting physically and emotionally close, to give members a chance to experiment with a new behavior, and to release "blocked" feelings. Guided fantasy, imagery, and other techniques intended to stimulate the imagination are utilized. (All this being said, I am mindful that the group members of Steve's dissertation are volunteers, and not individuals who are seeking therapy. I know that you will have to be "appropriate" to sustain the members' comfortableness in the experience over the eight sessions.)

3) A closing thought:

Just to reiterate, the videos and designated approaches looked fine. I'm just sending these few thoughts to encourage you to be mindful of the distinctiveness (juxtaposition) of the two groups. Outcome measures are more likely to have meaning when the groups looked significant different, perhaps because the facilitators/leaders operate out of the corresponding poles on a spectrum spanning the two designated approaches.

I hope this helps. If you have questions or need more or different feedback, please give me a call. Great work. . . and good luck!

Mark Minear, Ph.D.
Post Doctoral Fellow in Geropsychology
Knoxville VA Medical Center
Knoxville, Iowa

SCL-90-R Variables

APPENDIX L

SCL-90-R: Positive Symptom Distress Index   (Post Hoc Discovery)

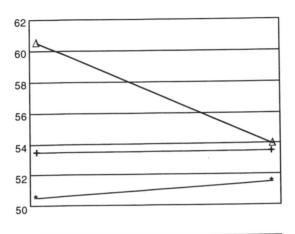

		Pre	Post
SLR	+	53.67	53.58
GLR	Δ	60.27	53.82
WLC	*	50.53	51.13

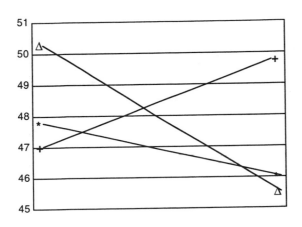

SCL-90-R: Hostility (Post Hoc Discovery)

	Pre	Post
SLR +	47.00	49.67
GLR Δ	50.09	45.45
WLC *	47.80	45.93

SCL-90-R: Interpersonal Sensitivity (Post Hoc Discovery)

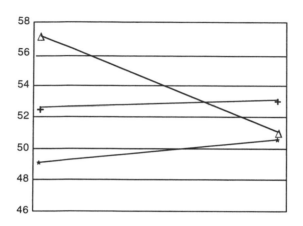

	Pre	Post
SLR +	52.33	53.50
GLR Δ	56.64	50.82
WLC *	49.33	50.73

SCL-90-R: Depression (Post Hoc Discovery)

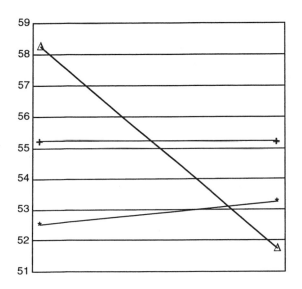

	Pre	Post
SLR +	55.33	55.17
GLR Δ	58.09	51.82
WLC *	52.47	53.20

SCL-90-R: Somatization (Post Hoc Discovery)

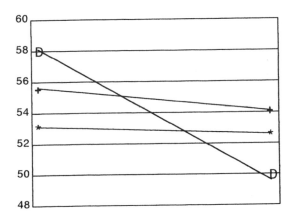

	Pre	Post
SLR +	55.50	53.92
GLR D	57.82	49.91
WLC *	52.93	52.47

References

American Association of Retired Persons (1994). *Reminiscence: Finding Meaning in Memories- Training Kit (D 13404)*. Program Coordination and Development Department. Washington DC: AARP.

American Association of Retired Persons (1995). *A Profile of Older Americans: 1995 (D 996)*. AARP Fulfillment, Program Resources Department. Washington DC: AARP.

American Psychiatric Association (1987). *The Diagnostic and Statistical Manual of Mental Disorders* (3rd ed. revised). Washington D.C.

American Psychiatric Association (1994). *The Diagnostic and Statistical Manual of Mental Disorders* (4th ed.). Washington D.C.

Arean, P. A., Perri, M.G., Nezu, A.M., Schein, R.L., Christopher, F., & Joseph, T.X. (1993). Comparative effectiveness of social problem-solving therapy and reminiscence therapy as treatments for depression in older adults. *Journal of Consulting and Clinical Psychology, 61*, 1003–1010.

Atchley, R.C. (1989). A Continuity theory of normal aging. *The Gerontologist, 29*, 183–190.

Ball State University 1996–1997 Directory *"B Book."*

Bailey, L.M. (1984). The use of songs in music therapy with cancer patients and their families. *Music Therapy, 4*, 5–17.

Beaulieu, E. & Karpinski, J. (1981). Group treatment of elderly with ill spouses. *Social Casework: The Journal of Contemporary Social Work. 62*. 551–557.

Beck, A.T. (1967). *Depression: Causes and treatments*. Philadelphia: University of Pennsylvania Press.

Beckham, K., & Giordano, J. (1985). Illness and impairment in elderly couples: Implications for marital therapy. *Family Relations, 34*.

Bergland, C. (1982). The life review process in geriatric art therapy: A pilot study. *The Arts in Psychotherapy, 9*,121-130.

Berlatsky, M.N. (1962). Some aspects of the marital problems of the elderly. *Social Casework: The Journal of Contemporary Social Work, 43*, 233–237.

Beutler, L.E. (1991). Have all won and must all have prizes? revisiting Luborsky et a.l's verdict.. *Journal of Consulting and Clinical Psychology, 59*, 226–232.

Boylin, W., Gordon, S.K., & Nehrke, M.F. (1976). Reminiscing and ego integrity in institutionalized elderly males. *The Gerontologist, 16*, 118–124.

Brok, A.J. (1992). Crises and transitions: Gender and life stage issues in individual, group, and couples treatment. *Psychoanalysis and Psychotherapy: The Journal of the Post Graduate Center for Mental Health, 10*, 3–16.

Bumagin, V.E., & Hirn, K.F. (1989). *Helping the Aging Family: A Guide for Professionals*. Glenview, Illinois: Scott, Foresman and Company.

Burnside, I. (1995). Chapter 11: Themes and props: Adjuncts for reminiscence therapy groups. In Haight, B.K. & Webster, J.D. (Eds.). *The Art and Science of Reminiscing: Theory, Research, Methods, and Applications*. (153–163). Washington, D.C.: Taylor and Francis.

Burnside, I. & Schmidt, M.G. (1984). *Working with the Elderly: Group Process and Techniques* (2nd edition). Montery, CA: Wadsworth Health Sciences Division.

Burnside, I. & Schmidt, M.G. (1994). *Working with the Elderly: Group Process and Techniques* (3rd edition). Boston: Jones and Bartlett Publishers.

Butler, R.N. (1974). Successful aging and the role of the life review. *Journal of the American Geriatrics Society, 22*, 529–535.

Campbell, D.T. & Stanley, J.C. (1963). *Experimental and Quasi-Experimental Designs for Research*. Chicago: American Educational Research Association/Rand McNally & Company.

Carlson, C.M. (1984). Reminiscing: Toward achieving ego integrity in old age. *Social Casework: The Journal of Contemporary Social Work,65*. 81–89.

Carson, V., Soeken, K.L., & Grimm, P.M. (1988). Hope and its relationship to spiritual well being. *Journal of Psychology and Theology, 16*, 159–167.

Carter, B. & McGoldrick, M. (1989). T*he Family Life Cycle: A Framework For Family Therapy*. (19–20). New York: Allen and Bacon.

Coleman, P.C. (1974). Measuring reminiscence characteristics from conversation as adaptive features of old age. *International Journal of Aging and Human Development, 5*, 281-294.

Coleman, P. (1994). Adjustment in later life. In Bond, J. (Ed.). *Ageing in Society: An Introduction to Social Gerontology*. (97–132). Thousand Oaks, CA: Sage Publications.

Conway, P. (1988). Losses and grief in old age. *Social Casework: The Journal of Contemporary Social Work. 69*. 541–549.

Corey, G., Corey, M.S., Callanan, P., & Russell, J.M. (1992). *Group Techniques*. (2nd ed.). Pacific Grove, CA: Brooks/Cole Publishing Company.

Crose, R. (1990). Reviewing the past in the here and now: Using gestalt therapy techniques with life review. *Journal of Mental Health Counseling, 12*, 279–287.

Crose, R. (1996). Individual consultation/private communication 6/14/96.

David, D. (1990). Reminiscence, adaptation, and social context in old age. *International Journal of Aging and Human Development, 30*, 175–188.

Davis, B. (1995). Chapter 20: Finding meaning in memories: the American Association of Retired Person's reminiscence program. In Haight, B.K. & Webster, J.D. (Eds.). *The Art and Science of Reminiscing: Theory, Research, Methods, and Applications*. (265–272). Washington, D.C.: Taylor and Francis.

DeGenova, M.K. (1992). If you had your life to live over again: What would you do differently? *International Journal of Aging and Human Development, 34*, 135–143.

Derogatis, L.R. (1994). *SCL-90-R (Symptom Checklist-90-R) Administration, Scoring, and Procedures Manual*. Minneapolis, MN: National Computer Systems, Inc.

Dietsche, L.M. (1979). Know your community resources: Facilitating the life review through group reminiscences. *Journal of Gerontological Nursing, 5*, 43–46. *appendix only*

Ellis, A. (1962), *Reason and Emotion in Psychotherapy*. Secaucus, NJ: Lyle Stuart.

Ellison, K.B. (1981) Working with the elderly in a life review group. *Journal of Gerontological Nursing, 7*, 537-541.

Erikson, E. (1963). *Childhood and Society*. New York: W.W. Norton.

Erikson, E. (1982). *The Life Cycle Completed: a Review*. New York: W. W. Norton & Company Inc.

Ernst, M. and Ernst, N.S. (1984). Functional capacity in Mangen, D.J. and Peterson, W.A. (Eds.). *Research Instruments in Social Gerontology (vol.3) Health, Program Evaluation, and Demography*. University of Minnesota Press: Minneapolis.

Fallot, R.D. (1980). The impact on mood of verbal reminiscing in later adulthood. *International Journal of Aging and Human Develooment, 2,* 385-400.

Feil, N. (1993). *The Validation Breakthrough: Simple Techniques for Communicating with People with Alzheimer's Dementia.* Baltimore, Maryland: Health Professions Press, Inc.

Fillenbaum, G.G. (1996). Private telephone conversation/ communication 7/3/96.

Frankl, V. (1959). *Man's Search For Meaning.* Boston, MA: Beacon Press.

Fritz, T. (1996). Individual consultation/private telephone communication 6/25/96.

Fry, P. S. (1991). Individual differences in reminiscence among older adults: Predictors of frequency and pleasantness ratings of reminiscence activity. *International Journal of Aging and Human Development, 33,* 311–26.

Gallagher, D.E. (1979). Comparative effectiveness of group psychotherapies for reduction of depression in elderly outpatients (Doctoral dissertation, University of Southern California, 1979). *Dissertation Abstracts International, 39,* 5550B. *appendix only*

Gallagher, D.E., Thompson, L.W., & Peterson, J.A. (1982). Psychosocial factors affecting adaptation to bereavement in the elderly. *International Journal of Aging and Human Development, 14,* 79–95.

Gilbert, J.P. (1977). Music therapy perspectives on death and dying. *Journal of Music Therapy, 14,* 165–171.

Gilewski, M.J., Kuppinger, J, & Zarit, S.H. (1985). The aging marital system: a case study in life changes and paradoxical intervention. *Clinical Gerontologist. 3* (3). 3–15.

Goldmeier, J. (1985). Helping the elderly in times of stress. *Social Casework: The Journal of Contemporary Social Work. 66.* 323–332.

Goldwasser, A.N., Auerbach, S.M, & Harkins, S.W. (1987). Cognitive, affective, and behavioral effects of reminiscence group therapy on demented elderly. *International Journal of Aging and Human Development, 25,* 209-222.

Gorey, K.M. & Cryns, A.G. (1991). Group work as interventive modality with the older depressed client: A meta-analytic review. *Journal of Gerontological Social Work, 16,* 137–157.

Greenberg, L.S., Rice, L.N., & Elliot, R. (1993). *Facilitating Emotional Change: The Moment-by-Moment Process.* New York: The Guilford Press.

Greenberg, L.S. (1994). *Integrative Psychotherapy - a Six Part Series: Part 5 - A demonstration with Dr. Leslie Greenberg.* Psychological and Educational Films. Corona Del Mar, CA.

Haase, R.F. & Ellis, M.V. (1987). *Multivariate analysis of variance. Journal of Counseling Psychology, 34*, 404–413.

Haight, B.K. (1984). The therapeutic role of the life review in the elderly. *Academic Psychology Bulletin, 6,* 287-289.

Haight, B.K. (1988). Excerpts from life review: Part I; A method for pastoral counseling. *Journal of Religion and Aging, 5.*

Haight, B.K. (1991). Reminiscing: The state of the art as a basis for practice. *International Journal of Aging and Human Development, 33,* 1–32.

Haight, B.K. & Dias, J.K. (1992). Examining key variables in selected reminiscing modalities. *International Psychogeriatrics, 4,* 279–290.

Haight, B.K. (1994). Reminiscence training supplement 5: Sample questions for conducting a reminiscence. inAmerican Association of Retired Persons. *Reminiscence: Finding Meaning in Memories- Training Kit (D 13404).* Program Coordination and Development Department. Washington DC: AARP.

Haight, B.K., Coleman, P., & Lord, K. (1995). Chapter 13: The linchpins of a successful life review: Structure, evaluation, and individuality. In Haight, B.K. & Webster, J.D. (Eds.). *The Art and Science of Reminiscing: Theory, Research, Methods, and Applications.* (179–192). Washington, D.C.: Taylor and Francis.

Haight, B.K. & Hendrix, S. (1995). Chapter 1: An integrated review of reminiscence. In Haight, B.K. & Webster, J.D. (Eds.). *The Art and Science of Reminiscing: Theory, Research, Methods, and Applications.* (3–21). Washington, D.C.: Taylor and Francis.

Ham, R.J. & Meyers, B.S. (1993). *Late Life Depression and Suicide Potential: A Physician's Guide to Identification and Treatment (D 15111).* Social Outreach and Support Section, Program Coordination and Development Department. Washington DC: American Association of Retired Persons.

Hargrave, T.D. & Anderson, W.T. (1992). *Finishing Well: Aging and Reparation in the Intergenerational Family.* New York: Bruner/ Mazel.

Heppner, P.P., Kivligan, D.M., & Wampold, B.E. (1992). *Research Design in Counseling.* Pacific Grove, CA: Brooks/Cole Publishing Company.

Holzberg, C.S. (1984). Anthropology, life history, and the aged: The Toronto Baycrest Centre. *International Journal of Aging and Human Development, 18,* 255-275.

Hsu, L.M. (1992). Chapter 5: Random sampling, randomization, and equivalence of contrasted groups in psychotherapy outcome research. In

Kazdin, A.E. (Ed.). *Methodological Issues & Strategies in Clinical Research*. (91–106) Washington, DC: American Psychological Association.

Huber, K. & Miller, P. (1984). Reminisce with the elderly-do it! *Geriatric Nursing, 5.*

Ingersoll, B., & Goodman, L. (1980). History comes alive: Facilitating reminiscence in a group of institutionalized elderly. *Journal of Gerontological Social Work, 2,* 305-319.

Instrumental ADL from Activities of Daily Living section of the Older Americans Resource Services (OARS) Multidimensional Functional Assessment Questionnaire in Fillenbaum, G.G. (1988). *Multidimensional Functional Assessment of Older Adults: The Duke Older Americans Resources and Services Procedures*. Hillsdale, N.J.: Lawrence Erlbaum Associates.

Janoff-Bulman, R. & Wortman, C.B. (1977). Attributions of blame and coping in the "real world": severe accident victims react to their lot. *Journal of Personality and Social Psychology. 35* (5). 351–363.

Jones, R.G. (1977). *Irrational Beliefs Test- A Test to Determine Excessive Expectations*. Test Systems International Ltd.

Junge, M. (1985). "The book about daddy dying": A preventive art therapy technique to help families deal with the death of a family member. *Art Therapy.* (3) 4–10.

Kerlinger, F.N. (1986). *Foundations of Behavioral Research (3rd ed.)*. Orlando, Florida: Holt, Rinehart and Winston, Inc.

Kessler, R.C., McGonagle, K.A., Zhao, S., Nelson, C.B., Hughes, M., Eshleman, S., Wittchen, H.-U., & Kendler, K.S. (1994). Lifetime and 12 month prevalence of DSM-III-R psychiatric disorders in the United States: Results from the National Comorbidity Survey. *Archives of General Psychiatry, 351,* 8–19.

Knight, B. (1986). *Psychotherapy with Older Adults*. Newbury Park, CA: Sage Publications, Inc.

Knight, B. (1992). *Older Adults in Psychotherapy: Case Histories*. Newbury Park, CA: Sage Publications, Inc.

Kubler-Ross, E. (1969). *On Death and Dying*. New York: Macmillan Publishing Company.

Langer, E.J. (1977). The illusion of control. *Journal of Personality and Social Psychology, 32,* 951–955.

Latour, W. (1996). Individual consultation/private telephone communication 6/27/96.

Lewis, C.N. (1971). Reminiscing and self-concept in old age. *Journal of Gerontology, 26,* 240–243.

Lewis, M.J., & Butler, R. N. (1974). Life-review therapy: Putting memories to work in individual and group psychotherapy. *Geriatrics, 29,* 165–173.

Liang, J. (1984). Dimensions of the Life Satisfaction Index A: A structural formulation. *Journal of Gerontology, 39,* 613–622.

Lowenthal, R. I. & Marrazzo, R. A. (1990). Milestoning: Evoking memories for resocialization through group reminiscence. *Gerontologist, 30,* 269–72.

Luborsky, L., Singer, B., & Luborsky, L. (1975). Comparative studies of psychotherapy. *Archives of General Psychiatry, 32,* 995–1008.

Mangen, D.J. and Peterson, (1984). Research Instruments in Social Gerontology (vol.3) Health, Program Evaluation, and Demography. University of Minnesota Press: Minneapolis.

Matteson M. A., & Munsat, E.M. (1982). Group reminiscing therapy with elderly clients. *Issues In Mental Health Nursing, 4,* 177-189. *appendix only*

McCarthy, S.V. (1985). Geropsychology: Meaning in life for adults over seventy. *Psychological Reports. 56* (2), 351–354.

McMahan, A.W. & Rhudick, P.J. (1964). Reminiscing. adaptational significance for the aged. *Archives of General Psychiatry, 10,* 292–298.

Molinari, V.,& Reichlin, R.E. (1985). Life review reminiscence in the elderly: A review of the literature. *International Journal of Aging and Human Development, 20,* 81–92.

Moody, H.R. (1988). Twenty-five years of the life review: Where did we come from? Where are we going?. in Disch, R. (Ed.). *Twenty-Five Years of the Life Review: Theoretical and Practical Considerations.*(7–24). New York: The Haworth Press, Inc.

Multidimensional Functional Assessment: The OARS (Older Americans Resources and Services) Methodology (2nd ed.). Appendix A, Center for the Study of Aging and Human Development, Duke University, 1978.

Naranjo, C. (1970). Present-centeredness: Technique, prescription, and ideal. In Fagan, J. & Shepherd, I.L. (Eds.). *Gestalt Therapy Now: Theory/ Techniques/ Applications.*(47–69). New York: Harper & Row, Publishers.

National Council on Aging/ Harris survey (1974) *(Myths and Realities of Aging in America).*

National Institute on Aging & National Committee to Preserve Social Security and Medicare. (1994). Depression: A serious but treatable illness. *Secure Retirement, 3,* 45–47.

Neugarten, B.L., Havighurst, R.J., Tobin, S.S. (1961). The measurement of life satisfaction. *Journal of Gerontology, 16,* 134–143.

Neugarten, B.K. (1974). Age groups in American society and the rise of the young-old. *Annals of the American Academy of Political & Social Science*, *415*, 187–198.

Norris, J.T., Gallagher, D., Wilson, A.B., & Winograd, C.H. (1987). Assessment of depression in geriatric medical outpatients: the validity of two screening measures. *Journal of the American Geriatrics Society, 35*. 989–995.

Paivio, S.C. & Greenberg, L.S. (1995). Resolving "unfinished business": Efficacy of experiential therapy using empty-chair dialogue. *Journal of Consulting and Clinical Psychology, 63*, 419–425.

Paul, G.L. (1967). Strategy of outcome research in psychotherapy. *Journal of Consulting Psychology, 31*, 109–118.

Peachy, N.H. (1992). Helping the elderly person resolve integrity versus despair. *Perspectives in Psychiatric Care, 28*, 29–30.

Peck, R. (1956) Psychological developments in the second half of life. In Anderson, J.E. (Ed.) Psychological Aspects of Aging. Washington, DC: American Psychological Association.

Perls, F.S. (1969). *Gestalt Therapy Verbatim*. Moab, Utah: Real People Press.

Perotta, P., & Meacham, J.A., (1981–82). Can a reminiscing intervention alter depression and self-esteem? *International Journal of Aging and Human Development, 14*, 23–30.

Polster, E. & Polster, M. (1973). *Gestalt Therapy Integrated: Contours of Theory and Practice*. New York: Vintage Books.

Rogers, C.R. (1957). The necessary and sufficient conditions of therapeutic personality change. *Journal of Consulting Psychology, 21*, 96–103.

Romaniuk, M., & Romaniuk, J. (1981). Looking back: An analysis of reminiscence functions and triggers. *Experimental Aging Research, 1*, 477–489.

Sagy, S. & Antonovsky, A. (1990). Explaining life satisfaction in later life: The sense of coherence model and activity theory. *Behavior, Health, & Aging, 1*, 11–15.

Scates, S.K.H., Randolph, D.L., Gutsch, K., & Knight, H.V. (1986). Effects of cognitive behavioral, reminiscence, and activity treatments on life satisfaction and anxiety in the elderly. *International Journal on Aging and Human Development, 22*, 141-146.

Schwartzberg, S.S. & Janoff-Bulman, R. (1991). Grief and the search for meaning: exploring the assumptive world of college students. *Journal of Social and Clinical Psychology, 10* (3). 270–288.

Seligman, M.E.P. (1990). Why is there so much depression today? In R.E. Ingram (Ed.). *Contemporary psychoanalytical approaches to depression.* (pp. 1–9). New York: Plenum.

Sherman, E. & Peak, T. (1991), Patterns of reminiscence and the adjustment of late life adjustment. *Journal of Gerontological Social Work, 16*, 59–73.

Shostrum, E. (1964). Three Approaches to Psychotherapy (*Part2: Fritz Perls, Gestalt Psychotherapy*).

Singer, V. I. (1991). Reminiscence group therapy: A treatment modality for older adults. *Journal for Specialists in Group Work, 16*, 167–171.

Slater, R. (1995). *Psychology of Growing Old: Looking Forward.* Bristol, PA: Open University Press.

Stevens, J.O. (1971). *Awareness: Exploring, Experimenting, Experiencing.* Moab, Utah: Real People Press.

Stevens, J. (1990). *Intermediate Statistics: A Modern Approach.* Hillsdale, New Jersey: Lawrence Erlbaum Associates, Publishers.

Stevens, J. (1996). *Applied Multivariate Statistics for the Social Sciences* (3rd ed.). Mahwah, New Jersey: Lawrence Erlbaum Associates, Publishers.

Sweney, A.B. (1996). individual consultation/private telephone communication 6/26/96.

Taft, L.B., & Nehrke, M.F. (1990). Reminiscence, life review, and ego integrity in nursing home residents. *International Journal of Aging and Human Development,*

Taylor, S.E. (1983). Adjustment to threatening events: a theory of cognitive adaptation. *American Psychologist, 38*, 1161–1173.

Taylor, S.E., Lichtman, R.R., & Wood, J.V. (1984). Attributions, beliefs about control, and adjustment to breast cancer. *Journal of Personality and Social Psychology, 46*, 489–502.

Thompson, S.C. (1985). Finding positive meaning in a stressful event and coping. *Basic and Applied Social Psychology, 6*, 279–295.

Thompson, S.C., & Janigian, A.S. (1988). Life schemes: a framework for understanding the search for meaning. *Journal of Social and Clinical Psychology, 7*, 260–280.

Tobin, S.S. (1991). Personhood in Advanced Old Age: Implications For Practice. New York: Springer.

Toseland, R.W. (1990). *Group Work Older Adults.* New York: New York University Press.

Toseland, R.W. (1995). *Group Work With the Elderly and Family Caregivers.* New York: Springer Publishing Company, Inc.

Trauptman, J., Eckels, E., & Hatfield, E. (1982). Intimacy in older women's lives. *The Gerontologist, 22*, 493–498.

U.S. Bureau of the Census. (1994). Statistical abstract of the United States: 1989 (114th ed.). Washington, DC: U.S. Government Printing Office.

Vickers, W.D. (1983). Project looking back: A structured reminiscence experience. *Activities, Adaptation, and Aging, 3*, 3 -38.

Viney, L.L., Benjamin, Y.N., & Preston, C. (1989). Mourning and reminiscence: Parallel psychotherapeutic processes for elderly people. *International Journal of Aging and Human Development, 28*, 239–249.

Walasky, M., Whitbourne, S.K., & Nehrke, M. F. (1983). Construction and validation of an ego integrity status interview. *International Journal of Aging and Human Development, 18*, 61–72.

Walsh, F. (1989). The family in later life . In Carter, B. & McGoldrick, M. (Eds.). T*he Family Life Cycle: A Framework For Family Therapy*. (312–327). New York: Allen and Bacon.

Waters, E. B. (1990). Life review: Strategies for working with individuals and groups. *Journal of Mental Health Counseling, 12*, 270–278.

Waters, E. B. (1995). Life Review: Strategies for Working With Individuals and Groups. Madison, WI: Brown & Benchmark.

Westgate, C.E. (1996). Spiritual wellness and depression. *Journal of Counseling and Development, 75*, 26–35.

Wolfelt, A.D. (1988). *Death and Grief: A Guide for Clergy*. Muncie, Indiana: Accelerated Development, Inc. Publishers.

Wolinsky, M.A. (1986). Marital therapy with older couples. *Social Casework: The Journal of Contemporary Social Work, 67*, 475–483.

Worden, J.W. (1982). *Grief Counseling and Grief Therapy. a Handbook for the Mental Health Practitioner*. New York: Springer Publishing Company.

Wortman, C.B. (1983). Coping with victimization: Conclusions and implications for future research. *Journal of Social Issues, 39*, 195–221.

Yalom, I.D. (1985). *The Theory and Practice of Group Psychotherapy*. (3rd ed.). New York: Basic Books.

Yesavage, J.A., Rose, T.L. & Spiegel, D. (1982). Relaxation training and memory improvement in elderly normals: Correlation of anxiety ratings and recall improvement. *Experimental Aging Research, 8*, 195–198.

Yesavage, J.A., Brink, T.L., Rose, Y.L., Lum, O, Huang, V., Adey, M., & Leirer, V.O. (1982). Geriatric depression scale. *Clinical Gerontologist, 1*, 37. ® 1982 The Haworth Press. Reprinted with permission.

Yesavage, J.A., Brink, T.L., Rose, T.L., Lum, O., Huang, V., Adey, M., & Leirer, V.O. (1983). Development and validation of a geriatric depression screening scale: a preliminary report. *Journal of Psychiatric Research, 17*. 37–49.

Yontif, G.M. & Simkin, J.S. (1989). Gestalt therapy. In Corsini, R.J. & Wedding, D. (Eds.). *Current Psychotherapies (fourth ed.)*. (323–362). Itasca, IL.: F.E. Peacock Publishers.

Zinker, J.C. (1978). *Creative process in Gestalt Therapy*. New York: Vintage Books.

Index